Fitness, Personal Care Services & Education

Daniel Lewis

MASON CREST

Mason Crest
450 Parkway Drive, Suite D
Broomall, PA 19008
www.masoncrest.com

Printed in the United States of America
First printing
9 8 7 6 5 4 3 2 1

Series ISBN: 978-1-4222-4132-5
Hardcover ISBN: 978-1-4222-4140-0

Library of Congress Cataloging-in-Publication Data is available on file.

Developed and Produced by Print Matters Productions, Inc.
(www.printmattersinc.com)
Cover and Interior Design by Lori S Malkin Design LLC

CAREERS IN DEMAND FOR HIGH SCHOOL GRADUATES

Agriculture, Food & Natural Resources

Armed Forces

Computers, Communications & the Arts

Construction & Trades

Fitness, Personal Care Services & Education

Health Care & Science

Hospitality & Human Services

Public Safety & Law

Sales, Marketing & Finance

Transportation & Manufacturing

KEY ICONS TO LOOK FOR:

 Words to understand: These words with their easy-to-understand definitions will increase the reader's understanding of the text while building vocabulary skills.

 Sidebars: This boxed material within the main text allows readers to build knowledge, gain insights, explore possibilities, and broaden their perspectives by weaving together additional information to provide realistic and holistic perspectives.

 Educational Videos: Readers can view videos by scanning our QR codes, providing them with additional educational content to supplement the text. Examples include news coverage, moments in history, speeches, iconic sports moments and much more!

 Text-dependent Questions: These questions send the reader back to the text for more careful attention to the evidence presented there.

 Research projects: Readers are pointed toward areas of further inquiry connected to each chapter. Suggestions are provided for projects that encourage deeper research and analysis.

CONTENTS

For millions of Americans, life after high school means stepping into the real world. Each year more than 1 million of the nation's 3.1 million high school graduates go directly into the workforce. Clearly, college isn't for everyone. Many people learn best by using their hands rather than by sitting in a classroom. Others find that the escalating cost of college puts it beyond reach, at least for the time being. During the 2016–2017 school year, for instance, tuition and fees at a "moderate" four-year, in-state public college averaged $24,610, not including housing costs, according to The College Board.

The good news is that there's a wide range of exciting, satisfying careers available without a four-year bachelor's degree or even a two-year associate's degree. Careers in Demand for High School Graduates highlights specific, in-demand careers in which individuals who have only a high school diploma or the general educational development (GED) credential can find work, with or without further training (outside of college).

These jobs span the range from apprentice electronics technician to chef, teacher's assistant, Web page designer, sales associate, and lab technician. The additional training that some of these positions require may be completed either on the job, through a certificate program, or during an apprenticeship that combines entry-level work and class time. Happily, there's plenty of growth in the number of jobs that don't require a college diploma, though that growth is fastest for positions that call for additional technical training or a certificate of proficiency.

So what career should a high school graduate consider? The range is so broad that Careers in Demand for High School Graduates includes 10 volumes, each based on related career fields from the Department of Labor's career clusters. Within each volume approximately 10 careers are profiled, encouraging readers to focus on a wide selection of job possibilities, some of which readers may not even know exist. To enable readers to narrow their choices, each chapter offers a self-assessment quiz that helps answer the question, "Is this career for me?" What's more, each job profile includes an insightful look at what the position involves, highlights of a typical day, insight into the work environment, and an interview with someone on the job.

An essential part of the decision to enter a particular field includes how much additional training is needed. Careers in Demand features opportunities that require no further academic study or training beyond high school as well as those that do. Readers in high school can start prepping for careers immediately through volunteer work, internships, academic classes, technical programs, or career academies. (Currently, for instance, one in four students concentrates on a vocational or technical program.) For each profile, the best ways for high school students to prepare are featured in a "Start Preparing Now" section.

For readers who are called to serve in the armed forces, this decision also provides an opportunity to step into a range of careers. Every branch of the armed forces, from the army to the coast guard, offers training in areas including administrative, construction, electronics, health care, and protective services. One volume of Careers in Demand for High School Graduates is devoted to careers that can be reached with military training. These range from personnel specialist to aircraft mechanic.

Beyond military options, other entry-level careers provide job seekers with an opportunity to test-drive a career without a huge commitment. Compare the ease of switching from being a bank teller to a sales representative, for instance, with that of investing three years and tens of thousands of dollars into a law school education, only to discover a dislike for the profession. This series offers not only a look at related careers but also ways to advance in the field. Another section, "Finding a Job," provides job-hunting tips specific to each career. This includes, for instance, advice for teacher assistants to develop a portfolio of their work. As it turns out, employers of entry-level workers aren't looking for degrees and academic achievements. They want employability skills: a sense of responsibility, a willingness to learn, discipline, flexibility, and above all, enthusiasm. Luckily, with 100 jobs profiled in Careers in Demand for High School Graduates, finding the perfect one to get enthusiastic about is easier than ever.

The Varied World of People Services

This book covers careers in personal care and services, fitness, and education—a broad area with lots of career possibilities. These careers can be great for people who like to work with other people or who like to work with their hands. Personal-care jobs are those jobs that involve care of other people's bodies, such as cutting hair, doing facials, or performing spa treatments. The fitness field includes all jobs involving exercise, such as teaching aerobics and yoga or working as a personal trainer. The field of education includes jobs for school aides and preschool aides who work in this field. Service careers also include jobs such as housekeeping and sewing. At the moment the personal care and service sector is a very good place to look for work.

Chapter 1 covers hairstylists and barbers. If hair interests you—if you like to look at pictures of hairstyles and spend hours coloring and styling your own and your friends' hair, or if you just like to see people looking neat and trimmed, then this career might be right for you. There are lots of opportunities available in all types of barbershops and salons, and if you become an expert stylist or colorist you can make a great income. You'll have to get a license and probably spend a couple of years learning your skills, but then you'll be in a growing field where you will meet new people every day. Be ready for competition, though; hair stylist Jet Rhys says of the field, "It's a big industry. You have to be up on your people skills and you have to look sharp."

If you like to spend your time in spas, then definitely check out Chapter 2, which discusses cosmetologists, skin-care specialists, makeup artists, manicurists, and other professionals who spend most of their time touching up and beautifying their clients. The word "cosmetology" can be a little confusing because it can actually cover a wide range of specialties, including hair styling, facials, massage, manicures, makeup, and other spa treatments. Some cosmetologists even end up in laser centers, zapping unwanted hair and wrinkles. If this field interests you, you should read Chapter 1 as well, because there are a lot of similarities between the two career areas. Like hair stylists, cosmetologists have to go to school and get licensed. The training is fastest if you pick just one specialty, such as manicures and pedicures, but you'll make more money if you can provide multiple services. Many cosmetologists specialize in several areas.

Are you an exercise fanatic? Do you spend all your free time in the gym? Do you have a daily yoga practice? Are you a black belt in karate? If so, turn to Chapter 3, which covers careers including fitness instructor, personal trainer, martial arts instructor, and yoga teacher. If you go into the exercise field, you'll get to spend lots of your time engaged in your favorite form of exercise; you'll have to keep in shape for your clients! During your working hours, you'll help clients exercise, either one-on-one or in a group class. You'll watch their form so that they get maximum benefit without hurting themselves. Every body has a unique build and different exercise needs, which is part of the attraction of the field to many practitioners. For example, yoga instructor Paula Lynch says, "There are so many different body types, some students have injuries or disabilities, and even some able-bodied students have more energy or mental blocks. It keeps me learning about the practice in new ways, learning how to apply the asana [pose] practice to specific students' needs." To improve in this profession and to keep up with trends, you'll go to seminars and workshops. This field is especially beneficial for anyone who wants to work evenings and weekends or who might want to work part time.

Do you like babies and toddlers? Do you find little kids irresistible? Then check out Chapter 4, which is on nannies, babysitters, and day care assistants. If you go into this field, you'll spend your workdays taking care of little tykes, from the tiniest newborns to kids nearly ready for kindergarten. If you work as a nanny or babysitter, you may also work with older kids after school, on weekends, and during vacations. You'll change diapers, sing lullabies, serve snacks, and clean up spills. You'll need endless patience, but your reward will be lots of little hugs and smiles.

Chapter 5 is about preschool aides and school aides. If you like working with kids but like them a bit older than babies and toddlers, you might enjoy this field. Schools of all levels need aides and assistants to help the main teachers with their daily work. As an aide you may greet kids in the morning, prepare materials for them to use in class, help them get lunch, and watch them at recess. This is a great field for anyone who wants to make a real difference in a child's life. This career is also a good stepping-stone for those who might want to become a teacher later on.

Are you a clean freak? Do you like to make a house neat and tidy? Chapter 6 would interest you—it's about housekeepers, maids, janitors, and other cleaners. You could work for a hotel, a hospital, or a school, or you could clean houses. This field is very easy to enter; you won't need any extra training as long as you're enthusiastic, strong, and can do the work.

You may never have considered a career as a funeral attendant, but you might after reading Chapter 7. People die every day, so there's a steady need for funeral workers. Funeral attendants do all kinds of jobs, from polishing limousines to collecting dead bodies from the morgue. You'll have to be neat, polite, and punctual—and be interested, rather than turned off, by human biology and the idea of dead bodies—if you want to succeed in this field. Funeral attendants insist that their job isn't at all grim or ghoulish. Funeral attendant Randy Clark says when he is helping to embalm a dead body, "I always like to think of the person being someone I love and care about." He adds that showing proper respect and care for the bereaved is another meaningful part of his job.

If you know how to sew and like it, you should consider a career as a seamstress, tailor, or upholsterer, discussed in Chapter 8. In these jobs you would measure people or furniture and cut and sew cloth to fit them precisely. All sewing careers are fairly difficult, and it takes several years to master these trades. But if you know the basics and are willing to learn, you can get a job doing simple sewing and gradually work your way up to a master craftsperson.

Most of these fields are not hard to enter, though many of them take years to master. Many of these jobs are deeply satisfying to their practitioners. Personal service jobs offer the

▲ Housekeeping and janitorial work doesn't require any extra training as long as you're enthusiastic, strong, and can do the work.

chance to make a real difference in someone's life, whether it be by caring for toddlers, giving a fabulous massage, letting a grieving spouse cry on your shoulder at a funeral, or running a great exercise class. In these fields you can often see the results of your work immediately, such as when you clean a filthy house or sew a perfect garment. If you have artistic ambitions, many of these fields offer numerous creative opportunities, from designing exercise

▲ If you want to be a personal trainer at a gym or health club, you'll need to get certified.

programs to dyeing a client's hair the perfect shade of red. And many personal service, fitness, and education jobs are great for anyone who wants a flexible schedule or would prefer to work part time. There are jobs in this area that could suit you—whether you're a people person or an introvert.

Opportunities in personal care and services, fitness, and education include some of the most plentiful and popular jobs in the country. If you think you'd like to help people, work with your hands, be creative in your work, or spend your days doing your favorite exercise, you should consider one of the careers profiled in this chapter.

Hairstylist/Barber

Keep up with the latest hair trends.
Make your customers look great. Perform
a vital service.

WORDS TO UNDERSTAND

commission: here, an amount of money paid for a particular transaction; often it's a percentage of the total value.

cosmetologist: a professional in the field of makeup and skin care.

facialist: someone who provides beauty treatments for the face.

utilitarian: describes something that's designed to be useful.

Hairstylists and barbers take care of people's hair. They style, cut, shampoo and condition, color, highlight, fit hairpieces, blow-dry, and arrange hair for special occasions. Today more than 670,000 people work as barbers, hairdressers, and **cosmetologists**; exciting opportunities exist for anyone who wants to dedicate themselves to mastering the latest trends. Beyond the creativity, cutting and styling hair is a great profession for anyone who likes to meet people, make customers feel great, and work a flexible schedule. You'll need to spend at least a few months training at a beauty or salon school and get a state license. Then you can be on your way to make your customers look fabulous.

◀ A colorist touches up a client's roots with hair dye.

Is This Job Right for You?

Answer the following questions to see whether a career as a barber or hairstylist is right for you.

Yes	No	1. *Are you fascinated by hairstyles?*
Yes	No	2. *Do you like to meet different people every day?*
Yes	No	3. *Can you work on your feet for hours?*
Yes	No	4. *Do you like to work with your hands?*
Yes	No	5. *Do you enjoy studying magazine fashion and hair trends?*
Yes	No	6. *Can you work well with other people?*
Yes	No	7. *Are you good at handling complaints and criticism?*
Yes	No	8. *Can you keep your work area neat and your tools sterile?*
Yes	No	9. *Are you good at listening to and following directions?*
Yes	No	10. *Do you feel comfortable working weekends and evenings?*

If you answered "Yes" to most of these questions, you may have what it take to be a hairstylist or barber. To find out more about these professions, read on.

What's the Work Like?

Barbers and hairstylists do basically the same work, but barbers tend to be male and serve a male clientele in basic surroundings. Hairstylists (either male or female) serve men and women and often create more elaborate cuts. Either way, you'll start by discussing the cut a client wants, perhaps looking at photos he or she has selected from magazines. You'll also evaluate the shape of your client's face and the texture of his or her hair so you can use the proper cutting techniques. In some salons, you may shampoo and condition your client's hair. In others, a shampooer or assistant will do it. Once the client is in your chair, wearing a salon robe or drape, you'll carefully trim or cut his or her hair using precise techniques as well as your own creative talents to give your client the look he or she wants.

TALKING MONEY

The average wage for hairstylists and cosmetologists is $11.66 per hour, according to 2016 data from the U.S. Bureau of Labor Statistics. Barbers' wages were slightly higher—about $12.38 per hour on average. Some high-end hairstylists earn more; the top 10 percent of hairstylists earned more than $25 per hour.

▲ Before a client sits in the chair, he or she will have their hair shampooed and conditioned. This makes it easier for hairstylists to make even cuts.

While you cut, you may also get to know your client or catch up. Your personal connection with your customers is essential to keeping them happy and turning them into steady customers. If you're cutting off several inches or more, you may suggest that your client donate the cut hair to Locks of Love. If your client requests hair color, such as highlights, or a chemical straightening process, you'll do the work before or after the cut, depending on what has been requested. In most salons, you'll also blow dry your client's hair. You may also recommend a product or two; commission on these sales may be an important part of your wages. Throughout the appointment, your expertise is essential to your customer's satisfaction.

If you're a barber, your work will be similar, though more straightforward. However, your customers may also ask for help in concealing full or partial hair loss, perhaps with a hairpiece. You may also trim beards, color hair, shave clients' faces, and perform simple facials. You'll sterilize your equipment and scissors, and keep your scissors sharp. Whether you're a barber or a stylist, do your job well, and you'll be on your way to building a base of steady clients.

▲ A Barbers may use scissors when cutting a client's hair; however, it is common for them to use electric razors, too. In some cases, a man may want to buzz his whole head, or keep the sides short and the top long.

Who's Hiring?

- A barbershop
- An owner-operated salon
- A salon that's part of a chain
- A spa
- Yourself

Where Are the Jobs?

Barbershops are typically **utilitarian** establishments. Some still have the traditional red-and-white striped barber pole out front. A barbershop may have several chairs all in a row next to each other facing a mirror. It will contain one or more sinks for shampooing customers, though not all barbershop customers want a shampoo.

A salon is usually more luxuriously decorated than a barbershop. The shampoo sinks may be in their own room. The chairs may be more separated than the ones in a barbershop to give clients more of a sense of privacy, though this isn't always the case. There will be changing rooms for clients who need to put on smocks before color treatments or perms. You'll spend some of your time around harsh chemicals, so you'll need to wear protective gloves and a smock.

Hair salons often offer services besides haircuts and treatments, and there may be a separate work area for manicurists, facialists, or makeup artists. You may find a hairstyling job at a spa, which will contain facilities for massages and other spa treatments. Barbershops and hair salons can be found in every location from a strip mall or shopping mall to a Victorian-style home on the main street of a small town to a corporate office building.

TALKING TRENDS

Employment opportunities for hairstylists, barbers, and cosmetologists are projected to expand by about 10 percent by 2026. Large numbers of barbers and hairstylists are self-employed. Flexible schedules are common, as is part-time work. Job opportunities are plentiful, but there is a lot of competition for the top jobs. If you're trained and licensed to provide multiple services, such as specialty cuts and coloring techniques, color correction, extensions, or special-occasion hairstyles, you'll be able to find better jobs and earn more money.

A Typical Day

Here are some highlights of a typical day for a hairstylist.

Give someone highlights and a cut. You spend an hour carefully gathering small sections of a customer's hair. You paint them with a bleach solution, wrap them with foil, set a timer, and settle your client under a heat lamp. While her hair lightens, you cut your next customer's hair. When the timer buzzes, you remove the foils, wash, trim, and blow-dry your client's hair. She leaves you a generous tip.

Whip up a wedding up-do. A bride arrives with her sister three hours before her wedding. You sweep up her hair into an up-do of gentle curls, fasten her veil, and carefully pull out a few wisps to match the photo she's brought you.

NOTES FROM THE FIELD

Hairstylist and business owner, San Diego, California

Q: *How did you get your job?*

A: When I was six years old I knew I wanted to do this. My parents wanted me to go to college, but I didn't want to. In my junior and senior years, I worked on my academic credits for a half day and took beauty school classes in the afternoon. When I finished my senior year, I received my high school diploma and my cosmetology diploma. Then I got an internship at Vidal Sassoon for 15 months, where I swept up, cleaned the bathroom, and brought in my own models to work on, all for minimum wage. Now I have my own hair salon.

Q: *What do you like best about your job?*

A: Being in a service industry and knowing that I have the proper training behind me, and the self-confidence to do the job well. You're serving people and you're making them feel good about themselves. You have such confidence when you're trained. You feel like, "I can do this, I can make this person over, I can fix this hair challenge."

Q: *What's the most challenging part of your job?*

A: Learning that you're not going to make everybody happy. You may think one way and they may think another. Communication with a client is the most challenging part of my job.

Q: *What are the keys to success to being a hairstylist?*

A: Staying current. You have to be well trained and you have to have positive energy. You have to have great listening skills, you have to sell yourself and your ideas, you have to be great at what you do, and you have to treat that client that's been coming to you for 10 years like it's the first time, every time.

Next comes the wind-down. After several more hair appointments, and dealing with one customer's complaint, you clean your station, sterilize your brushes, and check your supply of styling products to get ready for your next day.

▲ Many women have their hair professionally styled for their wedding day. Setting a client's hair with curlers, bobby pins, and hair spray helps to make the look special for the event.

Start Preparing Now

- Take hairstyling classes at high school.

- Study pictures of hairstyles in magazines and on TV.

- Get a job shampooing hair or cleaning up at a local salon.

- Practice the techniques you learn on your friends and family members.

Training and How to Get It

You'll have to get a license before you can work as a barber or hairstylist. What you'll have to do to get this license depends on your state. In most states you have to be at least 16 years old and have graduated from a state-licensed cosmetology or barber school. Some states require you to have a high school diploma. In others, finishing eighth grade is enough. To get a license, you have to pass a written test and demonstrate that you can cut hair, create certain hairstyles, sterilize and sharpen your equipment, and handle coloring and perm chemicals properly. If you move to another state, you'll have to get licensed again.

Though some vocational high schools offer courses in hairstyling, most people do their prelicense training at beauty school (also called hair or salon school) or barber school. You should check the school's course offerings to make sure it teaches exactly what you want to learn. To become a hairstylist or barber, you'll need to take courses in cutting hair, coloring hair, hairstyling, and health and safety. You could spend anywhere from several months up to two years taking classes. How long school takes often depends on how much time you can put in. Once you've graduated, you may have to work as an apprentice in a beauty salon or barbershop for a few months to more than a year. During this time, you'll perform cleanup duties and watch senior stylists work. You'll also practice your hairstyling skills, starting off with the simplest techniques and gradually working up to more difficult cuts and styles. Many stylists like to take continuing education courses to keep their skills current.

Learn the Lingo

Here are a few words you'll hear as a hairstylist or barber:

- **Extensions** Pieces of hair attached to a person's natural hair in order to make the hair appear longer; extensions can be attached with glue or metal rings or by braiding or weaving in the extension.

- **French twist** A hairstyle in which a woman's hair is twisted in a vertical roll and pinned at the back of her head.

- **Highlights** Light streaks in hair made by bleaching selected strands.

- **Lowlights** Dark streaks in hair made by dyeing selected strands.

- **Toupee** A term older men may use to refer to a hairpiece or partial wig worn to cover a bald spot.

Finding a Job

To find a job as a hairstylist or barber, start with your high school or cosmetology school's placement service. Some salons will place advertisements for workers in newspapers, on school bulletin boards, or online. If you really want to be good at what you do, you'll probably want to complete an internship at a major salon or hairstyling company. These internships can be very competitive, and it can take some persistence to land one. If at first you don't succeed, call back every month or so. When you get an interview, practice what you're going to say with family and friends before you go to the salon. When you go to the interview, look sharp and show up on time;

one of the biggest problems in the beauty industry are employees who fail to show up when they're scheduled. Tell the interviewer you want to be part of a team and work in a learning environment and that you'll do whatever it takes to be a great hairstylist.

 See what it's like to be a hairstylist.

You can also start building up your client base by working as a freelance stylist out of your home or apartment, offering cuts to friends and family members for a reasonable fee. If you're good they may rely on you. Then when you apply for a salon job, you may be ahead of the competition if you can demonstrate that you have your own "following" of customers.

Tips for Success

- Do your best to make your customers happy. The best source of new business is word of mouth, and the best clients are the ones who keep coming back because they love your work and can't imagine letting anyone else cut their hair. Customers tend to become extremely loyal to individual stylists.

▲ A barber shows his apprentices how to properly shave a client's beard.

- There are many different kinds of barbershops and salons; apprenticeships are a good opportunity to find the sort of establishment that is right for you.

Reality Check

Many salons pay their stylists on **commission** rather than salary. If you're paid on commission, the more regular clients you have, the more money you'll make. You may have to act like a salesperson, pushing clients to buy more services and products.

Related Jobs to Consider

Shampooer. You won't need any formal training or a license to get started washing and conditioning hair.

Stylist specializing in weaves and extensions. You'll study techniques that will enable you to create elaborate looks—especially braided styles, with real hair or extensions.

Cosmetologist. You'll do facials, manicures, spa treatments, and makeup.

How to Move Up

- Open your own salon or barbershop. If you run your own business, you'll take the lion's share of the profits. You'll also get to decide how to decorate, what products to carry, and who will work for you. To succeed, take courses in management, marketing, and business basics.

LEARN MORE ONLINE

CAREERS IN BEAUTY

This site offers information on careers in hairstyling and cosmetology. It also details grants and scholarships and schools throughout the country. It's associated with the American Association of Cosmetology Schools (AACS). http://beautyschools.org/careers-in-beauty/

PROFESSIONAL BEAUTY ASSOCIATION (PBA)

This association provides various services for beauty professionals, including advocacy, business help, and training. http://www.probeauty.org

MAKEUP ALLEY

Members contribute reviews of hair and beauty products and discuss hair care and other cosmetics topics. http://www.makeupalley.com

- Learn specialties. Hairstylists who can provide lots of different services make more money than those who just cut hair. Become a colorist or an expert in color correction. (Women will pay big bucks for stylists who can fix their home-coloring disasters.) Master the latest specialty haircutting techniques.

TEXT-DEPENDENT QUESTIONS

1. *About how many hairstylists, barbers, and cosmetologists are there in the United States?*

2. *What is the average hourly pay for a hairstylist?*

3. *What is a typical day like?*

4. *What is the PBA and what services does it offer?*

RESEARCH PROJECTS

1. *YouTube is a treasure trove of information about the latest techniques and hairstyles. Search for videos on different hair and makeup trends, and study how the looks are achieved.*

2. *Find out about beauty schools that are near you. Search for "beauty schools near me" or try https://www.beautyschoolsdirectory.com, and write down a list of the institutions you find. Look into each one more carefully: is it well reviewed? What do former students say about it? What courses are offered and how much do they cost? Which one feels the most right for you?*

Cosmetologist/Skin-Care Specialist/Makeup Artist/Manicurist

Make customers look and feel great. Work in a soothing environment. Beautify and improve faces, skin, and nails.

WORDS TO UNDERSTAND

destination spa: a type of resort that's focused on specialized spa treatments, such as one near a mineral spring.

oxygen facial: a type of treatment that involves spraying moisturizer onto the face with pressurized air.

rejuvenation: here, a practice or activity that makes someone feel or look younger or more vital.

Do you have a long-standing interest in makeup and nail polish? Would you happily spend your weekends in a spa? Do you have a knack for knowing how to make your friends look and feel good? Are you fascinated by the details of skin care products and regimes? You may be a natural cosmetologist. Cosmetology includes many specialties, such as hairstyling, skin care, makeup, manicures, waxing, and more. In fact, it's an ancient

◀ Cosmetology covers many different specialties. One of the most common careers within cosmetology is makeup artistry.

career. Ever since Cleopatra lined her eyes in black and the Greeks relaxed in fragrant baths, men and women have specialized in adorning, beautifying, and treating the face and body. Today cosmetology is a fast-growing field with plenty of opportunities. What's more, although cosmetologists can spend years learning their craft, you can enter the field after a few months of training.

Is This Job Right for You?

To find out if being a cosmetologist is right for you, read each of the following questions and answer "Yes" or "No."

Yes	No	**1.**	*Do you like to work with your hands?*
Yes	No	**2.**	*Are you comfortable having physical contact with people?*
Yes	No	**3.**	*Can you stand on your feet for eight hours a day?*
Yes	No	**4.**	*Are you careful and detail-oriented?*
Yes	No	**5.**	*Do you listen and follow directions well?*
Yes	No	**6.**	*Can you keep your work area clean and your tools sterilized?*
Yes	No	**7.**	*Are you good at handling criticism?*
Yes	No	**8.**	*Do you enjoy meeting new people every day?*
Yes	No	**9.**	*Are you good at managing time and keeping to a schedule?*
Yes	No	**10.**	*Are you interested in skin care and personal grooming?*

If you answered "Yes" to most of these questions, you may have the talent to pursue a career as a cosmetologist. To find out more about this job, read on.

What's the Work Like?

The term "cosmetologist" is really a catch-all word for anyone who works on appearances—doing hair, makeup, skin care, or nails. Some cosmetologists specialize in one or two areas, while others perform a range of different types of services. If you become a cosmetologist, you could specialize in haircuts, hair coloring, hair straightening or perms—all

TALKING MONEY

In 2016, the average cosmetologist earned about $11.66 per hour. Manicurists and pedicurists made $10.65 an hour on average, while skin-care specialists averaged $14.55 per hour.

the things that hairstylists do. You might also do facials, do hair removal, use simple massage techniques, or run tanning beds. You might be trained in manicures and pedicures. You might specialize in applying makeup. As a certified cosmetologist, you can have your pick of jobs.

Many spas now offer treatments such as **oxygen facials** or seaweed wraps. Some cosmetology programs provide training in these techniques. As a manicurist or pedicurist, you'll take care of fingernails and toenails. You'll file nails, trim cuticles, apply lotion to hands and feet, and polish nails in the latest colors. Some of your clients will want nail extensions. You'll have to be careful to keep your tools and water sterile so you don't spread diseases among your clients. As a skin-care specialist or esthetician, you'll perform facials. You'll look through a magnifying lens to scrutinize pores and extract blackheads. You'll apply chemical peels and perform microdermabrasions. You'll apply cleansers, toners, and moisturizers to the skin, often using special motions as you add and wipe off the products. You may remove unwanted hair with wax, tweezers, or other techniques. Some estheticians specialize in laser treatments, removing hair, treating cellulite, and doing skin rejuvenations. You'll talk with your clients about their needs and recommend skin-care products to them.

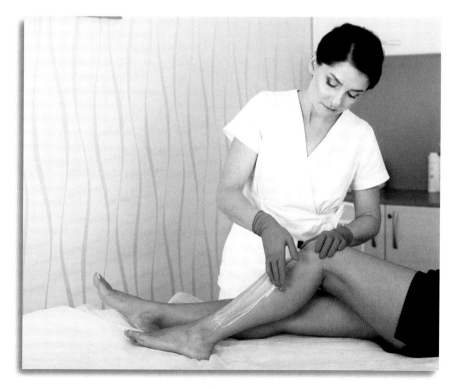

▲ An esthetician waxes a clients legs.

As a makeup artist, you'll learn how colors, glosses, powders, and liquid makeup work together to achieve daytime and evening looks for your clients. You'll learn the properties of many brands of makeup. You may work with clients who are on their way to special functions, such as proms or weddings. You may work in a theater or for a film studio.

Who's Hiring?

- A manicure/pedicure shop

- A beauty salon

- A department store

- A day spa or **destination spa**

- A specialty laser clinic

- A theater

- A film studio

Where Are the Jobs?

Most cosmetologists work in beauty salons, spas, or manicure shops. If you become a laser technician, you could work in a laser treatment center or a dermatologist's office. If you work in a salon, you'll spend your time around shampoo sinks, mirrors, and hairstyling equipment and supplies. You might do much of your work in a large room with several other employees and customers. You'll have to be polite and presentable at all times. Nail salons are often arranged in a similar way.

TALKING TRENDS

Demand for cosmetic workers is high and expected to increase as salon services gain in popularity and the number of day spas increases. Turnover in the field is also high, keeping up demand for employees. The U.S. Bureau of Labor Statistics predicts that employment among manicurists and skin-care specialists will grow faster than average between now and 2024. That said, competition will be fierce for the best-paying jobs at the most prestigious salons and spas.

▲ Make-up is not just for looking glamorous. It also plays an important role in movies and theater.

Smells can be very strong in hair salons or manicure shops. You'll have to be careful when handling hair dyes, hair straightening solutions, and nail polishes.

Some cosmetic treatments are done behind closed doors—clients may be naked or nearly naked for body waxes, tanning, and other body treatments, and it will be your job to protect their privacy. If you work with a laser, you'll have to remember to use eye protection so you don't burn your eyes.

As a makeup artist, you may work in a salon or a spa, preparing women for special occasions, such as proms, weddings, or photo shoots. Some makeup artists work at theaters or film studios, getting actors ready for their appearances.

A Typical Day

Here are the highlights of a typical day for a cosmetologist at a hair, nail, and tanning salon.

Make those tips tip-top. You arrive at work at 8:30 a.m. with three manicures on your schedule. You carefully sterilize your equipment after each client by immersing your tools in disinfectant; you throw away anything that can't be disinfected, including emery boards and orange sticks.

Set up for tanning. Your salon has two tanning beds in a back room. Two customers come to tan during their lunch break. You greet them, set them up in the tanning beds, carefully setting the lamps based in part on each client's skin type.

Make up the bride. You apply makeup to a bride for her evening wedding after your colleague arranges her hair. You go for the latest wedding look—a polished yet naturally dramatic effect. After your long day, you help clean the spa, check your supplies, and make a note to order new products.

Start Preparing Now

- Take high school cosmetology classes.

- Read articles about skin care and hairstyles.

- Practice doing your own face, facials, and nails. You can also practice on family and friends.

- Read up on different types of skin-care products and ingredients and what they do.

Training and How to Get It

Whatever specialty you choose, you'll need to spend at least three months going to cosmetology school. A general program in cosmetology will train you to do a variety of jobs. You'll study hair styling, hair coloring, makeup, skin care, and nail care. A full degree program in cosmetology can take two years or so; the required number of hours of education varies by state. You can also specialize in one area of cosmetics treatment, such as skin or nails. If you do this, your training could be much shorter than if you study all aspects of cosmetology; for example, a manicurist can be certified in just three or four months. Whatever your specialty,

NOTES FROM THE FIELD

Spa specialist, Seattle, Washington

Q: *How did you get your job?*

A: I moved from California back to Washington and was having a hard time finding a spa in Seattle to work in. A girlfriend of mine was familiar with Ummelin. She wrote a letter of recommendation for me, and I dropped off my résumé there.

Q: *What do you like best about your job?*

A: It gives me freedom to move from city to city, state to state, even country to country. I was very interested in moving around and experiencing different areas, and I was able to do this with my career decision. There are so many things to learn as far as continuing education. Also, it only took me one year to become licensed.

Q: *What's the most challenging part of your job?*

A: This job can be physically demanding on your body. You want to give so much to your clients, and they often need a lot of compassion and extra attention. I have found that people in this industry are healers and very giving. So at times it's easy to give too much of your energy to one person.

Q: *What are the keys to success to being a spa specialist?*

A: Technical skills [see "Training and How to Get It" for some examples of skills], good communication skills, being flexible, getting as much education in your field as possible, and having the passion to work with people and help them.

you'll have to get licensed in your state. You'll have to prove that you've taken the required number of hours of class time and then take a written and practical test to prove that you know the essential skills for your job.

▲ The job of a manicurist or pedicurist is all about precision. You must make sure that all nails are even and to the client's liking, and that nail polish is smooth.

As a skin-care specialist, you'll have to learn all about skin. You'll learn how to identify skin conditions, clean pores, extract blackheads, and massage skin to improve circulation. You'll practice doing chemical peels, eyebrow shaping, and waxing. You may take training in corrective makeup so that you can help people who have had skin surgery or laser treatments look better while they recover.

If you become a manicurist or pedicurist, you'll have to take a training course in nail health and maintenance. You'll practice treating nails and cuticles, shaping nails into attractive shapes, polishing nails, applying artificial nails or nail wraps, and nail art.

If you specialize in laser treatments, you'll have to take training courses on the particular lasers you'll be using. You'll practice assessing people's skin types, choosing laser settings that won't burn your clients, removing hair, doing facial **rejuvenation**, and postlaser skin treatment. Many cosmetologists take regular continuing education courses to keep up with trends in their fields and to learn new specialties. Clients will want the latest techniques and products in facials, hair removal, makeup, and spa treatment, so you may want to study aromatherapy, thalassotherapy (seawater treatments), specialty facial peels, herbal therapy, essential oil treatment, ear candling, body sugaring, nutrition, sun protection, mineral makeup artistry, or any number of other techniques.

Learn the Lingo

Here are a few terms you may hear in cosmetology work:

- **Electrolysis** A method of removing hair permanently by applying electricity to hair follicles.

- **Esthetics** The study of skin care, facials, cosmetics, waxing, and other areas, such as massage or reflexology.

- **Hot stone therapy** The process of placing hot stones on a customer's body to release tension.

- **Reflexology** The practice of stimulating pressure points on the feet to affect other parts of the body.

See what cosmetology school is like.

Finding a Job

There are lots of jobs available for cosmetologists and personal appearance workers. Many cosmetology schools will offer some service to help graduates find a position, and cosmetology businesses often contact schools if they need new employees. (A good placement service is one thing to look for in your training program.) You can also look for ads in the newspaper or online; search for "cosmetologist" plus your hometown.

Word of mouth and connections are the best ways to find jobs. If you have friends who work in the field, ask them about job openings. You can visit salons and spas in person and tell them you're a certified worker looking for a job. The best salons have many job applicants, and it can take a long time to land a job at a prestigious salon. Successful cosmetologists recommend extreme persistence if you want a job at a top spa; call the manager every month to see if there are any openings, describe your skills and interests, send holiday cards, and be flexible about what position you're willing to take.

If you get an interview, conduct a trial run with a friend before you go. Be sure to show up on time and be polite. Your prospective employer will want to know that you're reliable and will treat customers well. Try to look great yourself. If a salon offers you lousy hours or a job that's not your first choice, consider accepting the job anyway. You can always adjust your schedule or specialty after you've worked there for a few months.

Tips for Success

- Cosmetologists work with a great variety of customers. Some will want to have conversations while you work, and others will want to stay silent. If your client wants to talk, be sure you're a good listener; don't do most of the talking yourself!

- Remember, the looks you help someone create may not be lasting, but the experiences they have while all dolled up may stay with them.

Reality Check

Are you a good salesperson? Many spas expect their employees to sell products such as shampoo or makeup to customers. The cosmetologists who make the most money are often the ones who are also good at integrating sales pitches into treatment sessions.

Related Jobs to Consider

Hairstylist. If hair is your passion, you can specialize in cutting, styling, and treating hair.

Massage therapist. If you like to work in a more physical way, consider becoming a certified massage therapist. At a massage therapy school, you'll learn anatomy and techniques for releasing tension.

Cosmetic product salesperson. Cosmetics companies always need representatives to show off their products. You could travel to different salons selling shampoo and lotions, and you'd get free samples.

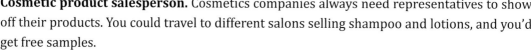

Tattoo artist or piercing specialist. Makeup and haircuts not permanent enough for you? Tattoo artists and piercers also get to enhance their customers' looks—for keeps!

How to Move Up

- Specialize. Cosmetologists who can perform specialty treatments, such as complicated facials, and who keep up with the trends get the best jobs at the best salons and spas. They also earn the best salaries and receive the highest tips. Similarly, become licensed in massage therapy. If you can perform facials and massages at a spa, you'll be in high demand.

- Open your own salon or day spa. If you have a good head for business, you could aim to open your own beauty business. As an entrepreneur, you can offer your choice of treatments, each customized to reflect your own tastes and beliefs. You can set your own prices and take a percentage of your employees' earnings.

TEXT-DEPENDENT QUESTIONS

1. *What are some of the specialties that fall under the umbrella of cosmetology?*

2. *What types of things do skin-care specialists do?*

3. *What training is required?*

4. *What are some related jobs you might consider?*

RESEARCH PROJECTS

1. *Find out more about how to care for skin. Research what role nutrition and sun exposure play in keeping skin healthy. Also find out more about skin-care regimens for people of ethnic backgrounds different from your own.*

2. *Look through fashion magazines (or search their online versions) for new trends in makeup design. Can you replicate those looks on yourself or your friends? Also check YouTube for tutorials in the latest styles.*

Fitness Trainer/Instructor

3

Help people shape up and lose weight. Promote inner balance and peace. Join a fast-growing field

WORDS TO UNDERSTAND

gyrotonics: a type of exercise regimen that includes a lot of circular movement.

Pilates: a type of exercise regimen focused on strengthening the body's core (meaning the abdomen, lower back, and hips).

weight training: a type of exercise regimen that uses dumbbells and other weights to improve strength.

Fitness workers help people exercise and move their bodies. They may work one-on-one with clients, customizing workouts for each customer, or they may teach large classes. Fitness workers oversee all sorts of movement and exercise techniques, including weightlifting, spinning, Pilates, yoga, and martial arts. The trends in fitness change constantly, so professionals must keep up-to-date. What's more, within many specialties, such as yoga, there are dozens of schools of techniques among which to choose.

In 2016, nearly 300,000 people worked as fitness trainers and instructors in the United States. American consumers, for example, spent more than $10 billion on yoga-related classes and products in 2016, according to the Yoga Alliance. Interest in fitness is expected to continue

◀ A fitness instructor creates a plan to help a client reach his goal.

to rise as Americans become increasingly health-conscious and interested in losing weight, staying flexible, and keeping toned. Exercise and fitness is a great field for someone with lots of energy and good people skills; it's also great for someone who wants a flexible schedule.

Is This Job Right for You?

Yes	No	1. *Do you enjoy physical activity?*
Yes	No	2. *Do you enjoy helping other people stay fit?*
Yes	No	3. *Do you enjoy learning about physical fitness and anatomy?*
Yes	No	4. *Are you patient?*
Yes	No	5. *Are you energetic?*
Yes	No	6. *Could you work evenings, weekends, or early mornings?*
Yes	No	7. *Are you organized and reliable?*
Yes	No	8. *Are you outgoing and willing to talk to strangers?*
Yes	No	9. *Can you keep up with changing fitness trends?*
Yes	No	10. *Are you healthy and strong?*

If you answered "Yes" to most of these questions, you may have the talent to pursue a career in fitness. To find out more about this profession, read on.

What's the Work Like?

Fitness workers help people exercise and take part in fitness routines, such as yoga. If you go into the fitness field, you may find yourself working with classes or individuals, putting them through their paces. Fitness instructors teach classes in any number of other activities that go in and out of fashion. If you work as a fitness instructor, you'll plan group classes that are fun and strenuous, but not too difficult. You may choose music to play during the class to increase your students' motivation. You'll demonstrate moves and then make sure the participants do them correctly so that they don't get hurt.

TALKING MONEY

The median income for fitness trainers and instructors is $38,160, according to 2016 data from the U.S. Bureau of Labor Statistics. Many fitness workers work part-time for an average of $18 an hour.

You'll be a combination drill sergeant and cheerleader, encouraging everyone to work hard.

Personal trainers work one-on-one with clients, customizing workouts to their clients' individual wants and needs. As a personal trainer, you may work with clients at a gym or in their homes. You'll actually stand over your clients as they exercise, encouraging them to new heights of performance. You'll track their progress and adjust the exercises as they get stronger.

As a yoga instructor, you may lead classes in yoga techniques as well as teach private students. You

TALKING TRENDS

The fitness industry is growing because people are increasingly concerned about optimizing their weight and gaining the physical and mental benefits of exercise. The U.S. Bureau of Labor Statistics predicts that people will spend increasing amounts on fitness services in the next 10 years as health concerns grow among aging baby boomers, parents put their children in health clubs to combat childhood obesity, and businesses implement health and fitness programs. The job outlook for this field is good—employment in the fitness field is expected to increase 10 percent by 2024, which is faster than average.

▲ Because form is so important, yoga instructors must make sure their students are doing the poses and breathing correctly.

▲ Martial arts instructors teach children and adults alike.

may specialize in a particular style of yoga, such as Ashtanga or Iyengar, or you may create classes that blend styles. You'll call out poses and demonstrate them. You'll help your students maintain correct breathing with their poses, and you'll lead them in a meditation or relaxation exercise at the end of class.

As a martial arts instructor, you'll teach adults and children martial arts techniques such as karate or aikido. You'll demonstrate all moves for your students and oversee their exercises and routines. You'll give occasional tests to see if your students have mastered enough skills to earn new belts.

Who's Hiring?

- Gyms and health clubs

- Yoga studios

- Martial arts schools

- Corporations with exercise programs

- Destination resort spas

- Yourself

Where Are the Jobs?

There are jobs for fitness instructors in all sorts of venues, including some you'd never expect. You could work anywhere from a health club to a fancy resort. Most fitness professionals work in gyms and health clubs. If you can teach classes such as aqua fitness, step aerobics, **gyrotonics**, or another kind of fitness class, you should be able to find a job at a health club. You may find jobs at several different health clubs; it's common for fitness instructors to teach at more than one location every week, especially if they work for a health club that has several branches in one city. Yoga teachers, martial arts instructors, Pilates teachers, and other specialized instructors can work at general health clubs or at specialized studios.

Health clubs aren't the only employers that will want to hire you. Corporations, rehabilitation centers, cruise ships, luxury spas, and island resorts all need fitness instructors and trainers to work with employees or guests. If you like visiting people in their homes, personal training might be a great option for you. Personal trainers often make house calls to motivate and train time-squeezed clients. Fitness work can also be a great career if you want to work at home—if you become a personal trainer, yoga instructor, or Pilates teacher, you can have your clients visit you in your own home studio.

▲ An aqua fitness instructor teaches a class at a resort.

A Typical Day

Here are the highlights of a typical day for a fitness instructor.

Get up and go. You have to teach two pre-work aerobics class at a health club. You get up at 5:30 a.m. and get to the club by 6:20 a.m. to get ready for your 6:30 a.m. class.

Make the morning rounds. You spend the morning circulating in the health club's weight room, helping clients choose weights and correcting their weight-lifting technique. You finish at noon.

Teach yoga in the evening. At 6 p.m. you teach a yoga class at a downtown yoga studio. You arrive at the studio at 5:50 p.m. to start your music and set up your mat. Class ends at 7:30 p.m., and your workday is over. You go to bed early so you can get up for the early aerobics class tomorrow.

Start Preparing Now

- Try a variety of styles of exercise, including **weight training**, aerobics, other health club classes, martial arts, running, or whatever else appeals to you. When you know what you like, you may decide to specialize.

- Work out at the gym, lift weights, run, and ride bikes.

- Take a wide variety of phys ed and health-club classes.

- Establish a personal yoga practice. Go to specialty yoga workshops.

- Practice your martial art daily. Improve your skills and earn higher belts.

- Read books and magazines about your fitness interests: bodybuilding, karate, yoga, Pilates, aerobics, etc.

- If your school offers them, take classes in human anatomy, muscle and skeletal groups, and exercise science.

- Volunteer to assist teachers in exercise, yoga, or martial arts classes.

Training and How to Get It

You'll need your high school diploma. Certification in first aid and cardiopulmonary resuscitation (CPR) is a good idea. Then you may need to get a certification from a fitness organization to prove to prospective employers that you're qualified to teach some kind of

NOTES FROM THE FIELD

Yoga instructor, New York, New York

Q: *How did you get your job?*

A: Yoga Works offers one of the most comprehensive yoga training programs, so I started by committing to their 500-hour training, which I did over the course of two years.

Q: *What do you like best about your job?*

A: I love connecting with people on different levels and helping students understand themselves a little better through their yoga practice. I see the body as an amazing vehicle through which we can access the deeper layers of ourselves; teaching asana [poses] allows me to present students with the challenge of connecting their bodies with their breath and tapping into the subtle and energetic layers of the self. We can learn so much about ourselves simply by threading our movements with our breath and listening to how the body responds. I feel really fortunate to be able to help students find this connection and humbled by how much I continue to learn from the students and the practice.

Q: *What's the most challenging part of your job?*

A: I am both challenged and inspired by all the different people that come to yoga. The diversity of students presents challenges and lessons for me in teaching. It keeps me learning about the practice in new ways: how to apply the asana practice to specific students' needs and to invite students not to feel frustrated by what they may not be able to do yet, but what they can explore in their body and breath each time they practice.

Q: *What are the keys to success to being a yoga instructor?*

A: It is imperative that as a teacher you do your own practice with regularity, integrity, and devotion. Good training is also very important, and to be continually learning on your own is essential.

exercise. Most health clubs won't give you on-the-job training, so you'd better know what you're doing when you start.

If you want to teach fitness classes at a gym or health club, you may be able to find work without getting certified. Health clubs mainly want to know that you can plan and lead a class. The best training includes taking lots of exercise classes yourself so that you know how a good class should be run. Getting certified is probably a good idea, though. Lots of health clubs require certification, and you'll be able to earn more money. To get certified, you have to pass a written test on human physiology and exercise techniques; there may be a practical test, too. Some certifying organizations offer training courses. There are many organizations offering certification, including the Aerobics and Fitness Association of America (http://www.afaa.com) and the American Fitness Professionals Associates (http://www.afpafitness.com). Once you've got a job as a fitness instructor, you can take seminars and workshops to improve your knowledge.

If you want to be a personal trainer you'll also have to get certified. Several organizations offer training programs and certification exams.

If you plan to teach yoga or martial arts you may not need certification. Martial arts disciplines often allow advanced students to start teaching. The yoga world has no formal certification requirements for teachers. If you're serious about teaching yoga, though, you ought to take a teacher training program. Many studios offer teacher training; look for one recognized by the Yoga Alliance (http://www.yoga alliance.org). Programs range from weekend workshops to year-long courses that require several hundred hours of work. Pilates instructors likewise do not necessarily need certification. However, the Pilates Method Alliance now offers certification as a way of ensuring quality control; they're a good place to look for teacher training programs (http://www.pilatesmethodalliance.com).

Learn the Lingo

Here are a few words you'll hear as a fitness worker:

- **Body mass index (BMI)** This is a measurement of a person's weight in proportion to his or her height; the lower the BMI, the leaner the person is.

- **Certified personal trainer** A health and fitness professional who has received specific training and has passed

Find out more about becoming a fitness trainer.

an exam to show his or her competence to create exercise programs to help people achieve their fitness goals.

- **Human physiology** The study of how the human body works.

Finding a Job

Lots of fitness trainers find jobs through word of mouth. If you have friends who work in the fitness industry, ask them about job possibilities. If you exercise at a health club and would like to work there, go see the manager and ask for a job application. Volunteer to help teach at your yoga studio or martial arts studio—it could lead to a paying job. Look for advertisements in the local newspaper or online on job sites. Do an Internet search for "personal trainer" or "fitness instructor" plus your hometown. You never know who might be looking for someone. Universities often advertise for fitness workers. You can sometimes find job announcements on bulletin boards at colleges. The AFPA and other organizations have job boards on their Web sites.

If you want to work as a group instructor, you will interview with the manager of the gym or studio to which you are applying. However, if you're a personal trainer you might interview directly with your clients. When you go to an interview, dress in neat clothes; casual or exercise clothing is

▲ If your goal is to teach classes at a gym or health club, take lots of exercise classes yourself so that you know how a good class should be run.

generally appropriate for interviews at gyms and studios, as long as it's not revealing or ratty. You may have to teach a sample class. If so, arrive on time, dressed to teach in clothing suited for your specialty. Tell the employer all about your experience and training in the fitness field, emphasizing your specialty. Show your enthusiasm and pleasant personality. Remember, the employer will want you to make customers want to keep coming to the gym and to bring all their friends, too!

LEARN MORE ONLINE

AMERICAN COUNCIL ON EXERCISE
This organization certifies personal trainers and fitness instructors. http://www.acefitness.org

NATIONAL STRENGTH AND CONDITIONING ASSOCIATION CERTIFICATION COMMISSION
This organization is just for strength-training specialists. https://www.nsca.com

YOGA ALLIANCE
This organization certifies yoga teachers and runs yoga training programs. http://www.yogaalliance.org

Tips for Success

- Smile! People want to work out with a trainer or instructor who makes them feel good. When you teach, try to make your classes or training sessions fun as well as strenuous.

- Never single anyone out for negative comment—that's embarrassing, and clients hate it.

Reality Check

Are you confident about your personal appearance? You'd better be. When you teach fitness classes, groups of strangers will watch your every move. As a personal trainer, you'll be very close to your clients when you assist them. Good personal grooming is a must!

Related Jobs to Consider

Recreation worker. You'll organize recreational programs for communities, cities, churches, summer camps, theme parks, or tourist attractions. There's lots of summer and part-time work in this field.

Assistant coach. You'll help a sports coach run team practices and games. This is a great job for a high school athlete.

Referee/umpire. Sports leagues always need people who can referee games. Only try this if you don't mind fans yelling at you.

How to Move Up

- Become a fitness manager. To manage a gym or studio, you'll likely need an associate's degree in fitness management.

- Become a physical therapy assistant. Physical therapy is growing as fast as fitness work, and physical therapy technicians can earn good money. You'll need to go to a community college to get an associate's degree, but working as a personal trainer is a great way to get started.

- Get a college degree in exercise science or physical education. This will allow you to get a job teaching physical education in a school or college, which can be a more secure job than working part-time in health clubs.

TEXT-DEPENDENT QUESTIONS

1. *Roughly how many fitness instructors and trainers were there in the United States in 2016?*

2. *What are some of the different exercise regimens that people use?*

3. *Do you need to be certified to be a fitness trainer?*

4. *What are some secrets to success in this field?*

RESEARCH PROJECTS

1. *If you are interested in this job at all, you are probably already physically active. But consider what types of exercise you've never done and try those out. If you've never tried yoga, take a class; if you've never lifted weights, get together with someone who has and try it out. What do you think of these regimens? Even if you don't like them, consider why other people might. (Take care of yourself—don't try anything dangerous and make sure you have guidance from people who know what they are doing.)*

2. *Choose a particular exercise regimen that interests you (such as yoga, Pilates, or aerobics) and research its history. How did it develop? When did it become popular and why do you think that occurred?*

Nanny/Babysitter/Day Care Assistant

4

Care for babies and toddlers. Watch little ones grow and change daily. Get and give lots of hugs.

WORDS TO UNDERSTAND

cardiopulmonary resuscitation: an emergency procedure to restore breathing or heartbeat.

entrepreneur: a person who starts his or her own business.

milestone: an event that indicates a new stage in development.

Do you like babies? Does the idea of spending your day surrounded by toddlers and little kids appeal to you? Child care is a growing field with plenty of opportunity. A growing number of parents need babysitters, nannies, or other child care professionals to watch their children when they work. Most of today's families have both parents in the workforce or are headed by a single working parent. According to the U.S. Bureau of Labor Statistics, almost three-quarters of all women with children of any age were in the labor force, and more than 60 percent of mothers with young children worked.

Babysitting or working in a day care center is a great way to see the world from a child's-eye view. It also offers a fascinating opportunity to watch babies grow through unique stages and learn to express themselves. Though turnover is high, many child care professionals wouldn't

◀ A day care assistant helps students with their artwork.

trade their position for the world. Dedicated child care workers share one common trait: They really love children and enjoy caring for them.

Is This Job Right for You?

To find out if being a child care worker is right for you, read each of the following questions and answer "Yes" or "No."

Yes	No	**1.** *Do you do really like babies and toddlers?*
Yes	No	**2.** *Are you very patient and loving?*
Yes	No	**3.** *Are you creative?*
Yes	No	**4.** *Do you like taking care of children?*
Yes	No	**5.** *Are you outgoing and energetic?*
Yes	No	**6.** *Are you good at inventing and leading games?*
Yes	No	**7.** *Are you okay with doing repetitive tasks, such as reading the same book repeatedly or changing diapers every couple of hours?*
Yes	No	**8.** *Do you enjoy watching babies and small children grow and develop?*
Yes	No	**9.** *Are you thorough about sanitation and cleanliness?*
Yes	No	**10.** *Can you stay calm when children are crying or throwing tantrums?*

If you answered "Yes" to most of these questions, you may have the talent to pursue a career as a babysitter, nanny, or day care assistant. To find out more about these jobs, read on.

What's the Work Like?

Child care workers, including nannies, babysitters, and day care workers, take care of small children when their parents can't. If you find a job as a nanny or babysitter, you'll care for the children of a single family in that family's home. You'll play with the kids, dress them, bathe them, change

TALKING MONEY

The average child care worker earns about $10.18 an hour, or an average of $21,170 per year, according to 2016 data from the U.S. Bureau of Labor Statistics. The highest-paid child care workers earn more than $15 per hour. A majority of nannies and babysitters work part-time and do not receive benefits.

▲ A nanny often works for one family. Here, a nanny helps her family's children decorate eggs for Easter.

their diapers or help them use the toilet, read them books, and supervise their naps. Depending on your hours, you may even put them to bed at night. You'll make and serve them meals, from bottles to real food. Some parents will expect you to do some light house-cleaning. You will also enforce your employer's rules. For instance, your children may not be allowed to watch television—some parents are very particular about this. If you care for school-age kids, you may pick them up after school and shuttle them around to activities and sports practices.

Day care workers handle larger groups of kids in age-segregated groups. If you work at a day care center, you will probably be assigned to one group of children, such as the older babies (crawlers and walkers who would run all over smaller infants) or the two-and-a-half-year-olds. The number of children will determine how many coworkers you have; states require specific ratios of child care workers to children, depending on the age of the

▲ A day care assistant reads a book to her students.

kids. Experts recommend low ratios of children to caregivers because children do best if they have plenty of adult attention.

As a day care worker, you'll greet parents and children, feed babies or get snacks and lunches for older kids, and repeatedly teach simple lessons such as "We share," or "We help." You'll also change diapers or monitor toilet runs, run or help with playtime, leading songs and hand games, overseeing the dress-up and other play areas. You'll also settle children down for their naps.

Who's Hiring?

- A day care center

- A family

- A corporation

- A church

- A community center

- An after-school program

Where Are the Jobs?

If you work for a family as a nanny, you'll probably spend a good portion of your workday in that family's home. You'll take care of the family's babies or toddlers while the parents go out to work. You'll spend most of your time in the children's bedrooms or playrooms, but you may go around the rest of the house and yard. Some rooms may be off limits to you and the kids. You'll be around valuable items, and you'll have to prove to the parents that you're trustworthy and won't steal their things. The parents may give you a house key and teach you the code for their security system so that you can come and go during the day. They may also lend you a car to use for taking children to appointments and playdates.

The majority of child care workers are employed by various types of day care centers. These businesses usually have several rooms for children of different ages. Most day care centers group kids by age so toddlers aren't in the same room as infants. Infant rooms contain cribs so the babies can take their naps. Toddler rooms often have a closet full of cots or mats for naptime. All rooms will have age-appropriate toys. The center will probably have some small tables and tiny chairs for lunch and snacks. It will have changing tables for diapering babies and tiny toilets for potty "trainees." Most day care centers have an outdoor playground with miniature playground equipment. You'll spend lots of your time outside supervising playing children.

A Typical Day

Here are the highlights of a typical day for a day care assistant in the infant room.

Greet parents and babies. Between 7:30 a.m. and 8:30 a.m., as parents drop off their babies, you and your coworker in the infant room offer the children and their parents a warm welcome. You hear who has sniffles and who's teething, and you listen to the special instructions

NOTES FROM THE FIELD

Day care assistant, *Austin, Texas*

Q: *How did you get your job?*

A: I was hired to fill in for my sister's position for the summer. I was going to leave when she returned. But I loved my job and the people who run Children's Discovery Center loved me, and they asked me to stay as a full-time teacher.

Q: *What do you like best about your job?*

A: I love the big smiles and hugs from each of my lovebugs every day.

Q: *What's the most challenging part of your job?*

A: Not letting myself get frustrated over simple, little basic things, such as when I try to accomplish too many tasks at one time. It's also hard when my babies move up to the next classroom!

Q: *What are the keys to success to being a day care assistant?*

A: Have patience! I have to remember that these are still small children who are learning about this big environment they are in each day. Remember it's okay to "take five" to stay alive. If you don't you will get burned out quickly. Your heart and mind have got to be a big part of why you are there.

a few parents pass along. You help them place their babies in their assigned cribs or bouncy seats. You also place bottles of formula and breast milk labeled with each baby's name in the refrigerator.

Help with feeding time. At 10:00 a.m. you put bottles in a bottle warmer; when they're tepid, you and your colleague start feeding the six babies in the room. Three can hold their own bottles. You feed two of them baby food from jars. After eating, everyone gets a fresh diaper.

Facilitate rest and play. Most of the babies sleep for the next two hours; you rock one who is having trouble falling asleep. After nap time you put mats on the floor for baby playtime. You roll a ball back-and-forth to one baby who can sit up, and hold another on your lap while you read a picture book. You put the three oldest babies in a wagon and take them for a ride around the block while your colleague sings to the other three, who are playing with infant gyms. Just before pickup time, you give the afternoon bottles and change diapers again.

Start Preparing Now

- Babysit.

- Volunteer in your church or community center nursery.

- Take courses on **cardiopulmonary resuscitation** (CPR) and child care.

- Take courses in child development, if your high school offers them.

- Visit your high school career counselor to get information on careers in child care.

- Read books, magazines, and Web sites about babies and children.

Training and How to Get It

Though your job may not require you to have training, any training you can get will put you ahead of the competition and make you a more knowledgeable, professional child care worker. Many babysitters and nannies learn how to take care of children by helping at home with their own brothers and sisters or other children of relatives. Others gain experience babysitting in middle school and high school or helping out at their church nurseries. Try to take at least some courses on child development and **milestones** . There are a lot of myths about babies. For instance, did you know that babies can't be spoiled? A good child development course will clear up many of these myths. Similarly, it's also important to know the latest safety information about babies. Did you know that it's dangerous to put an infant to sleep on his or her stomach? Courses can also teach you how to keep babies and toddlers happy and safe at each stage of development. No amount of training, however, can take the place of patience and kindness.

Some states have licensing requirements for child care workers in day care centers. You may need to prove that you've graduated from high school; some states will require you to take specialized courses at a community college. Some employers will want you to earn a credential such as child development associate (CDA) or certified child care professional (CCP). To get a CDA credential, you'll need to have a high school diploma or equivalent, have 480 hours of experience working with children in the past five years, and take 120 hours of formal child care courses. The CCP credential requires 720 hours of work and 180 hours of education; you'll also have to create a portfolio that shows what you can do, be observed by a more experienced teacher, take an exam, submit parental evaluations, and pay a fee.

If you drive children to their school or lessons, you'll also need a driver's license. Most employers will want you to get certified in first aid and CPR. In these courses, offered by your local Red Cross, you'll learn how to bandage small injuries and how to tell

▲ Although not a requirement for all day care workers, it is a good idea to be certified in CPR, especially when working with infants and toddlers.

when a child should see a doctor. You'll also learn emergency techniques such as how to resuscitate a child who has stopped breathing or how to help a child who is choking. There are many child care skills that you'll either learn from your employer or through experience, such as proper diapering procedures. Most day care centers will require you to wear disposable gloves and sterilize the changing table between changes to avoid spreading diseases. You'll learn how to heat bottles for small infants and how to feed older babies and children. You'll have to learn how to entertain your charges, which can be quite a challenge! It can take several weeks or months to get completely comfortable with caring for babies and toddlers.

Learn the Lingo

Here are some terms you hear working in the field of child care:

- **Cardiopulmonary resuscitation (CPR)** A first aid technique used on a person who has stopped breathing and whose heart may have stopped beating. Techniques for infants and children differ from CPR techniques for adults.

- **Caregiver** Here, a person who takes care of a child or children.

- **Early childhood development** The way babies and toddlers grow and develop in their first years. All children acquire certain skills, generally within a given time frame. For example, most babies start walking between 10 and 16 months, with a few stragglers waiting until 18 months.

 See what it takes to be a day care worker.

Finding a Job

Many nannies and babysitters find jobs through word of mouth. Tell your friends and acquaintances that you want to work as a babysitter, and chances are a family will call you out of the blue asking you to work for them. You can also make a flier and post it at schools or workplaces with bulletin boards, or run advertisements in community or group newsletters. As you gain experience and references, you should be able to find one or two families that can offer you full-time employment or substantial part-time work. Some nannies and babysitters work through agencies, however. A nanny service may want you to hold some certifications or at least have a high school diploma.

If you want to work at a day care center, look for ads in your local newspaper's classified section. You can also visit day care centers in person to introduce yourself to the owners or managers. Turnover is high in the industry so chances are good that you'll find an opening. If you don't, consider volunteering a few hours a week in a day care center, so that the day care director can observe your work and attitude firsthand.

However you go about finding a job, show your prospective employer that you're reliable, punctual, and friendly. Show up on time for an interview. Show your genuine interest in the children and the job. You'll need to provide references and perhaps undergo

▲ Job listings for nannies, babysitters, and day care assistants can be found online. Web sites, like care.com, are a good place for future caregivers to post their résumés and information for families or facilities that might employ them.

a criminal check. Before you look for a job, ask previous employers or teachers if they would be willing to answer questions about you and your work habits.

Tips for Success

- Share anecdotes with parents. Moms and dads love to hear about what their child did each day. Make a mental note (or write down) an observation for each child you care for, such as something funny she said or a new achievement he is working on. The parents you work for will be grateful.

- As your charges age out of your care, new clients will fill in if you have a good rapport with other parents in the community.

LEARN MORE ONLINE

INTERNATIONAL NANNY ASSOCIATION
This is a good spot for would-be nannies to look for information. http://www.nanny.org

NATIONAL ASSOCIATION FOR THE EDUCATION OF YOUNG CHILDREN
If you're interested in early childhood education, this is a good resource. http://www.naeyc.org

NATIONAL CHILD CARE ASSOCIATION
This group offers licenses to child care providers. http://www.nccanet.org

ZERO TO THREE
This Web site provides information on various topics of baby and child development. http://www.zerotothree.org

Reality Check

No one goes into child care work expecting to get rich, and you shouldn't either. The pay is low, and most workers don't get benefits, such as health insurance. The hours can be really long, too, and some centers are too busy for the workers to take breaks.

Related Jobs to Consider

Preschool aide. If you like working with kids but think you might prefer older kids, consider assisting the teacher at a preschool, kindergarten, or elementary school.

Nurse's aide. You'll work in a hospital or clinic, helping nurses take care of patients. If you work for a pediatric clinic, you'll assist babies and little kids.

How to Move Up

- Be an **entrepreneur**. Open your own day care center or nanny/babysitting service, or become a manager/administrator of a day care center. You'll select employees who will take care of other people's children, either at your own day care center or in clients' homes. You'll need a good head for business and excellent customer service skills. You'll need to be state-certified as well.

- Become a teacher's assistant. You'll still get to work with kids, but you won't have to do the heavy lifting required of a classroom teacher.

- Become a teacher. There are lots of opportunities for teachers at all levels, from preschool up to high school. You'll have to get a bachelor's degree, but you'll be around kids and make a real difference in their lives. You'll also get summer vacation time.

- Become a social worker or social work assistant. Social workers need at least a bachelor's degree, and more typically, a master's. However, social work assistant positions are easier to get and require only an associate's degree. Depending on your job placement, you may have a great deal of contact with children, and lots of opportunities to help people.

TEXT-DEPENDENT QUESTIONS

1. *What percentage of mothers with young children are in the labor force?*

2. *What kinds of tasks do day care workers do?*

3. *What might you do to start gaining experience in this job?*

4. *What are some secrets to success in this field?*

RESEARCH PROJECTS

1. *Get started on preparing for this career by taking a first-aid course, such as those offered by the Red Cross. See http://www.redcross.org/m/phssmrd/take-a-class for more information.*

2. *The more you know about child development, the better child care you'll be able to provide. You can start learning about milestones online (for example, the Centers for Disease Control and Prevention has good information here: https://www.cdc.gov/ncbddd/childdevelopment/index.html). You can also read some books on the subject, such as* **Child Development: A Practitioner's Guide** *by Douglas Davies and* **Ages and Stages** *by Charles E. Schaefer. Your school or local librarian may have additional suggestions.*

▲ Working with young children requires a lot of patience, but for the right person, it can be very fulfilling.

Preschool Aide/ School Aide

5

Spend your days working with kids. Make a real difference in a child's life. Be part of a teaching team.

WORDS TO UNDERSTAND

compensation: pay or other benefits provided in exchange for labor.

paraprofessional: someone who is assigned particular tasks but isn't licensed to do the entire job.

Preschool aides and school aides—also called "paras" (for **parapro-fessional**), teacher aides, or "assistants"—spend their days helping classroom teachers with their daily work. In 2016, there were more than 1.3 million school aides working in the United States. Recent federal laws require some schools to hire additional teaching aides, so the job out-look for aides is positive. It's especially good for anyone with two years of college, who speaks a foreign language, who has training in caring for students with disabilities, or who is willing to work in schools with high poverty levels. Working as a preschool or school aide is a wonderful job for anyone who enjoys children and wants to be part of an educational team.

◀ Working as a school aide is a great opportunity for someone who enjoys working with children and helping them learn.

Is This Job Right for You?

To find out if being a preschool or school aide is right for you, read each of the following questions and answer "Yes" or "No."

Yes	No	**1.** *Do you enjoy working with children?*
Yes	No	**2.** *Are you patient?*
Yes	No	**3.** *Are you organized and reliable?*
Yes	No	**4.** *Are you neat and do you know how to keep a room clean?*
Yes	No	**5.** *Are you good at classroom activities and projects?*
Yes	No	**6.** *Can you follow directions well?*
Yes	No	**7.** *Can you communicate clearly with both children and parents?*
Yes	No	**8.** *Do you like to organize games and activities for groups of children?*
Yes	No	**9.** *Are you good at solving problems?*
Yes	No	**10.** *Are you comfortable using a computer?*

If you answered "Yes" to most of these questions, you may have the talent to pursue a career as a teacher aide. To find out more about this job, read on.

What's the Work Like?

If you work as a teacher or preschool aide, you could find yourself doing almost any job you can think of. Teacher aides and preschool aides help classroom teachers, performing various necessary jobs so that teachers have more time to teach and plan lessons. In many cases, aides do nearly the same jobs as teachers. Some aides help with lessons and classroom work. Others do mostly nonacademic work, such as monitoring playgrounds and cafeterias.

If you become a school aide, you may spend much of your time helping students with their lessons. You may read stories; help children read, write, or work out their math problems; or supervise art projects. The teacher may put you in charge of keeping the classroom stocked with supplies. You

TALKING MONEY

Many preschool and school aides work part time, and their compensation **depends a great deal on experience, region of the country, and budget of the particular school. The average salary for teacher aides was $25,410 in 2016, according to the U.S. Bureau of Labor Statistics.**

▲ Helping students with their homework is part of the job of a school aide.

may take attendance, collect homework, and grade papers. If you're good with computers, you may be put in charge of the class computer lab.

The younger the children at the school, the more attention they will need. If you work at a preschool, you'll have to help the children get dressed to go outside and watch them closely while they play. You'll probably tie dozens of shoes every day, and you may have to dry occasional tears. You may even have to mop up "accidents." If you work at an elementary school or a middle school, the students will look up to you as a role model. You may have to enforce discipline, perhaps inspecting bathrooms or breaking up playground fights. Special-needs students may demand lots of your time; you may work one-on-one with a special-needs student who requires help with every activity, including feeding, dressing, and boarding the school bus.

Who's Hiring?

- Public schools, kindergarten through 12th grade

- Private schools, kindergarten through 12th grade

- After-school programs

- Summer programs

- Special teaching centers

- Public or private preschools

- Child care centers

- Religious organizations

TALKING TRENDS

There are always jobs available for teacher aides and preschool aides. However, the biggest demand over the next few years will be for special education aides and aides who speak a foreign language.

Where Are the Jobs?

School aides work in—you guessed it—schools. Preschool aides work in preschools, which are often much smaller than elementary schools. Preschools usually have brightly colored decorations on the walls and classroom toy collections in addition to preschool "work" materials, a small playground, and child-sized furniture. School aides work in public elementary, middle, or high schools, or in special education centers. If you work in a school, you may stay in a single classroom, or you may move from class to class or to the computer lab or library as you are needed. You may drive students in a school van. If you work with special-needs students, you may be assigned to a single student who requires assistance all day long. During the summer, you may have some flexibility. Many preschools stay open all year, so you may continue working during the summer. However, the summer routine may include more outdoor activities and wading pools or sprinklers—wear sunscreen! If you work at a public or private school, you may be able to find jobs in a summer program, or you may use the summer to take classes and improve your educational credentials.

A Typical Day

Here are the highlights of a typical day for a preschool aide.

Start the day early. You'll get to school around 7:30 a.m. to make sure everything is in place before the children arrive. When they do you'll greet them and their parents, help them hang up their coats, and get them settled in an activity center for free play before "circle time" starts.

Help with lessons. You'll assist children with developmental activities, such as learning their colors, using blocks to create patterns and buildings, and predicting what's going to happen next as you read a story aloud. During recess, you'll supervise playground fun. At lunch, you'll help the children get their lunches and drinks.

▲ A preschool aide might help students with a wooden shapes puzzle.

Help with naps and play. After supervising nap time, you'll give the children a snack and then take them outside to play until their parents arrive. One child's parent is late, and you reassure her: "Mommy will be here soon." Once everyone's gone, you'll reorganize the classroom and help set up for the next day.

See what it's like to be a teacher's aide.

Start Preparing Now

- Work with children. Babysit, volunteer with your church or community child care centers, help coach sports teams, or get a job at a summer camp.

- Get certified in first aid and cardiopulmonary resuscitation (CPR).

- Take classes in child development or early childhood education.

- Work on your reading, writing, math, and computer skills.

- Learn what your state requirements are to become a school aide.

Training and How to Get It

Most preschools will hire aides who have a high school diploma. Some of them will want you to have several months' experience working either with children or in some other job that shows that you're a responsible employee. You'll probably need a valid driver's license and a current first aid and CPR certification. You'll need to be healthy and strong; preschool aides spend a lot of time sitting on the floor, lifting children, mopping and vacuuming, and running around the playground.

School aides in K–12 schools usually need more training than preschool aides. Different states and school districts have different requirements, but many of them will want you to

▲ If you are a school aide working in a K–12 school, you may require more training or schooling. Sometimes, school aides will grade papers or exams; so you'll need to have a working knowledge of the subject material that is being taught.

NOTES FROM THE FIELD

Preschool aide, *Greenville, South Carolina*

Q: *How did you get your job?*

A: My friend was working at a Montessori preschool that had a job opening. She asked me if I'd be interested, and I'd never worked with kids before. But I came in and interviewed and got the job.

Q: *What do you like best about your job?*

A: I enjoy the one-on-one work, like teaching sandpaper letters to the kids individually. In the Montessori method, the children can choose to have a lesson, and they can keep doing it or choose to do something else. I also like playing with the kids and observing them. They're very interesting, the way they are with their friends and other people.

Q: *What's the most challenging part of your job?*

A: Patience! It comes and it goes, I guess, but you always have to be patient. Explaining things is hard, too. Sometimes you have to tell a child not to do something and then explain why they can't, and it can be hard to make them understand.

Q: *What are the keys to success to being a preschool aide?*

A: It's important to enjoy kids, to like playing with them. You have to make the kids comfortable in their environment, so they'll have more of an open mind and be interested in what you can teach them or whatever they choose to learn.

have at least some college training and several months' experience working in child care. If you actually help teach children, you will need more college than if you just supervise playtime and lunch. If you work with special needs children, you'll have to take classes in caring for the disabled. If you want to work at a Title I school—a school with a large number of students from low-income households—you will have to have a two-year degree or higher, to have attended at least two years of college, or to pass a local test proving that you can do the job. Some states require school aides to take a 30- or 40-hour training course to become certified. In many states you'll have to pass a test, such as ParaPro (an assessment of your reading, writing, and math skills), to comply with the requirements of the federal law No Child Left Behind.

Once you start working as a school or preschool aide, you'll receive lots of on-the-job training, for instance, in organizing class materials, teaching methods, keeping records, running a school, and operating computers and audiovisual equipment. Your school district might also give you time away from work to take classes in education and may even pay your tuition in exchange for your continuing to teach for a certain length of time. Warning: almost all preschools and schools will run a criminal background check on you before giving you a job. Stay out of trouble!

Learn the Lingo

Here are some terms you will hear working as a preschool aide or school aide:

- **Education paraprofessional** A paraprofessional is a person who provides support and assistance to a professional. School aides of various types, including teacher aides, special education assistants, bilingual assistants, and preschool aides, are often called education paraprofessionals.

- **No Child Left Behind Act (NCLB)** This is a federal law passed in 2002 that sets standards for school performance. It requires all school aides who work in the classroom to be "highly qualified."

- **Montessori** This is an educational method used in many preschools. Montessori schools encourage children to work independently and to practice life skills, such as washing dishes. It avoids tests, grades, and competition.

Finding a Job

Start by looking for advertisements searching for preschool or school aides. An Internet search for "preschool aide," "school aide," or "teacher assistant" plus your hometown may turn up several job openings. You can also simply contact the local schools that interest you. Send them a letter introducing yourself and expressing your interest in working as an aide. Include a high school transcript and any college transcripts you have, a résumé that lists your work experience (including any volunteer work you've done with children) and two or three people the school can contact for recommendations. If you've prepared lesson plans, you can include them in the package as well. When you go to a school for an interview, dress nicely and arrive on time. Convince the prospective employer that you're reliable, enthusiastic, and pleasant to work with.

▲ Montessori classrooms emphasize life lessons. Here, a school aide sits with a student as she plays with educational toys.

If you're not sure a job as a school aide is right for you, you can try working as a substitute aide. This way you can see what it would be like to work with different ages and abilities of students, including special needs students.

Tips for Success

- Don't take conflicts personally. Preschool aides often field complaints from parents about problems the children have at school. Just listen and nod; don't try to argue or convince the parents that they're wrong.

- Get help when you need it. Lead teachers and other staff will often have experience of some job issue you're facing or of something similar to a situation that is challenging you with one or more of the children. Draw from their experience. One day you may be the one with advice to share.

Reality Check

Teacher aides and preschool aides work hard for low pay. Don't expect to make lots of money. You may not get benefits such as health insurance, either; about 40 percent of school aides work part time for an hourly wage without benefits.

Related Jobs to Consider

Library or media assistant. You'll work in the library or media center, helping students find research materials and use computers, and bringing audiovisual materials to classrooms for teachers.

School secretary. You'll work in the school office, greeting visitors, and helping out behind the scenes.

Playground or cafeteria assistant. If you can't or don't want to take the classes to get certified for classroom work, you can find a job watching students at recess, at lunch, or after school.

LEARN MORE ONLINE

AMERICAN FEDERATION OF TEACHERS
This is the federal teachers' union Web site. It has pages for paraprofessionals such as aides, including a list of certification requirements by state. http://www.aft.org

NATIONAL EDUCATION ASSOCIATION
This national organization provides information for teachers, aides, parents, and others interested in education. http://www.nea.org

How to Move Up

- Become a preschool or school teacher. Many preschool and school aides go to college part time, taking classes in early childhood or elementary education. You can become a preschool teacher with a two-year associate's degree. A four-year education degree will make you eligible for teacher certification.

- Specialize. Some schools use specialized educational methods, such as the Montessori method. Special-needs teachers who can take care of children with disabilities are in high demand. Many schools need teachers and aides who can speak foreign languages. Any kind of specialty training will increase your job opportunities and earning potential.

TEXT-DEPENDENT QUESTIONS

1. What is a paraprofessional?

2. What kinds of tasks do preschool teachers' aides do?

3. What training is required for this job?

4. What are some related jobs you might also consider?

RESEARCH PROJECTS

1. Find out more about the ParaPro assessment. The Web site of the Educational Testing Service offers information and study guides to get you started (https://www.ets.org/parapro/test_prep/materials/). Learn the requirements and take a practice test to see if you're ready: https://www.teacherstestprep. com/parapro-practice-tests.

2. To make yourself more valuable to schools, start learning a foreign language. If you are not already learning a language at school, you can start learning for free with apps like Duolingo or busuu.

Housekeeper/Janitor/ Maid/Cleaner

6

See immediate results of your effort. Start work with minimal training. Make your clients' homes or offices look great

WORDS TO UNDERSTAND

gratification: satisfaction.
prospective: potential.
punctual: on time.

The cleaning field is one of the largest occupational fields in the United States. There are tons of jobs available in a huge range of workplaces. After all, every business, school, hospital, and hotel needs a cleaning staff, and millions of homeowners pay for housecleaning. The entry requirements are low; you can start work the day after you finish high school, or earlier. The money's not bad, and the job provides immediate **gratification**; you can see the difference your effort makes right away. If you don't mind hard physical work and want to get started earning money right away, this might be the field for you.

◀ **A housekeeper replenishes towels and soaps and replaces sheets for hotel guests.**

Is This Job Right for You?

To find out if being a janitor or maid is right for you, read the following questions, and answer "Yes" or "No."

Yes	No	1. *Do you like to clean things?*
Yes	No	2. *Do you enjoy housework and cleaning duties?*
Yes	No	3. *Are you strong and healthy?*
Yes	No	4. *Can you work on your feet for many hours at a time?*
Yes	No	5. *Can you sustain hard physical effort?*
Yes	No	6. *Can you follow directions well?*
Yes	No	7. *Can you work well either alone or on a team?*
Yes	No	8. *Do you like to work evenings or part-time?*
Yes	No	9. *Are you honest and trustworthy?*
Yes	No	10. *Are you **punctual**?*

If you answered "Yes" to most of these questions, you may have the talent to pursue a career as a janitor or maid. To find out more about these jobs, read on.

What's the Work Like?

Janitors, maids, housekeepers, and other cleaning professionals perform a range of necessary tasks to keep the world's businesses, schools, and homes clean, sanitary, and running smoothly. Maids and housekeepers sweep, mop, dust, vacuum, and polish. If you work at a hotel, you'll remove and replace sheets and towels, scrub bathtubs and bathroom floors, clean toilets, and stock rooms with soap, shampoo, and lotion. In a luxury hotel, you'll turn down sheets and leave mints on pillows, and restock the minibar. If you work at a hospital, you'll have to help keep the work environment sterile by disinfecting bed frames and mattresses and washing everything with germ-killing cleaner. If you work in an office building, you'll probably have a rolling cart for your cleaning supplies. Your tasks may

TALKING MONEY

Janitors average $24,190 a year, or $11.63 per hour; housekeepers and maids earn an average of $23,840 a year, or $11.46 per hour; and building cleaning workers earn an average of $30,960 a year, or $14.88 an hour, according to 2016 figures from the U.S. Bureau of Labor Statistics.

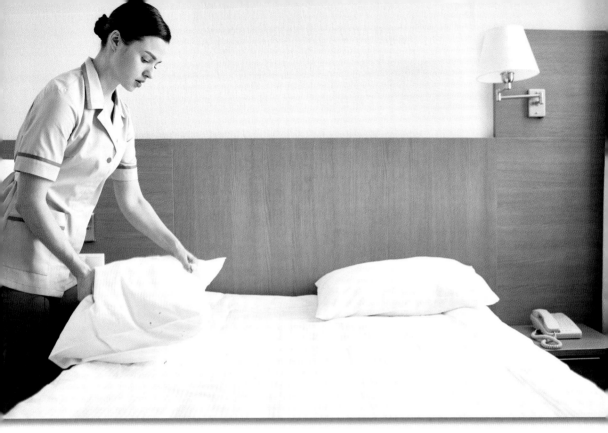

▲ As a hotel housekeeper, you will replace sheets for patrons who are staying at the hotel or for incoming guests.

include cleaning toilets, stocking toilet paper and paper towels, mopping or vacuuming floors, washing windows, emptying trash, and dusting shelves. If you work in houses and apartments, your jobs may include washing dishes, clothes, and bedding; putting away laundry; making the beds; cleaning ovens; polishing silver; and running errands, such as taking clothes to the dry cleaner. As a janitor, your work will include some heavier cleaning. You may shampoo rugs, wash walls, and move furniture. You may have to do minor repairs to faucets, lights, or air conditioners. You may have to spray for insects or trap rats.

Regardless of where you work, you'll probably be exposed to harsh chemicals. However, this is changing as some cleaning services specialize in eco-friendly cleaning techniques. They perform the usual cleaning services but use only biodegradable cleaning products. Such services are becoming more common as consumers grow more concerned about the environment.

If you become the supervisor of a team of housekeepers, you'll tell the workers what jobs they need to do and inspect their work when they're finished. You may have to fill out paperwork or electronic forms to report on your team's daily work.

▲ For larger facilities, such as schools, hospitals, or office buildings, a team of cleaners are needed. They will clean windows and floors and empty wastebaskets. They may have to move furniture to clean the hard-to-reach places.

Who's Hiring?

- Schools—from elementary schools to universities

- Local or state governments

- Stores and shopping malls

- Cleaning service companies

- Hospitals

- Hotels

- Corporations with office buildings

- Entertainment businesses, such as theaters

- Individual homeowners

Where Are the Jobs?

Cleaning professionals can work nearly anywhere. You may work in clients' houses, doing cleaning for specific families. If you want to clean houses, you can either work for yourself and have your clients pay you directly, or you can work for a maid service (often as part of a team). When you go into people's homes, you'll have to be extra careful not to break anything; most people feel nervous about letting strangers into their homes, and they may look to you first if something in the house gets broken or goes missing.

Lots of cleaners work in office buildings. You'll clean the hallways, bathrooms, conference rooms, and individual offices. Most office cleaning happens at night, when companies

TALKING TRENDS

There are always openings for janitors and housekeepers. There should be steady growth, especially in residential cleaning, as a growing number of families and working parents face a shortage of time for tasks such as cleaning, and also as an aging population loses the interest in and capacity for cleaning.

▲ Most cleaning crews begin working after the daytime office workers have left. They will vacuum or mop the floors, polish the furniture, and clean the windows to be sure it's clean for the next day's work.

NOTES FROM THE FIELD

Maid, Van Nuys, California

Q: *How did you get your job?*

A: I got my job through the newspaper. I took the job as a temporary thing, but once I got into it I realized that it was good money and that it was something I enjoyed doing, so I made it my career and I've been doing it ever since.

Q: *What do you like best about your job?*

A: What I like best is the feeling of satisfaction from doing a good job. I get a very good feeling when I see a big smile from a client after a job well done. I like to have a client's approval of my work. I also like that when I do a good job I receive wonderful gifts of appreciation for my work. Another thing I like is my celebrity clientele; I get to meet famous people I would probably not get to meet at any other job.

Q: *What's the most challenging part of your job?*

A: Most challenging is the feeling I get when I have to go to a new house and I don't know the client, how the house is, or how the client will receive me. Another challenge is not knowing how dirty a house is until you see it. A client might tell you one thing over the phone, but when you arrive it's completely different. I just have to do the best job I can.

Q: *What are the keys to success to being a maid?*

A: I think the keys to success to being a maid are to love what you do, have a good personality when it comes to dealing with people, take pride in what you do, and do good work so you can get referrals for more work.

are closed. You could also work in a school, cleaning hallways, lunchrooms, offices, and classrooms. Most school janitors work during the day, though classrooms can only be cleaned when school is not in session. If you work in a hospital, you'll clean hallways, lobbies, offices, patients' rooms, and even operating rooms. Hotel maids clean public spaces, such as lobbies, restaurants and gift shops, and individual hotel rooms and bathrooms. Some of your work may take place outside, in gardens and on walkways.

A Typical Day

Here are the highlights of a typical day for a maid who works for a cleaning service.

Start at the office. You arrive at your service's office at 8 a.m. to get your assignment for the day. You load your cleaning supplies into a van, and you and two coworkers drive to your first house.

Clean from top to bottom. You have three hours to clean your first house. You and your partners divide the jobs; you take the kitchen, the living room, and the downstairs bathroom. You load the dishwasher, scrub down the counters, sweep, mop, clean the windows, clean the faucet and other metalwork, and move on to the next room.

Go to house number two. You stop for a brief fast-food lunch, and then you drive to your next house. After you finish there, you drive back to your office, unload the van, and turn in your paperwork from the two houses.

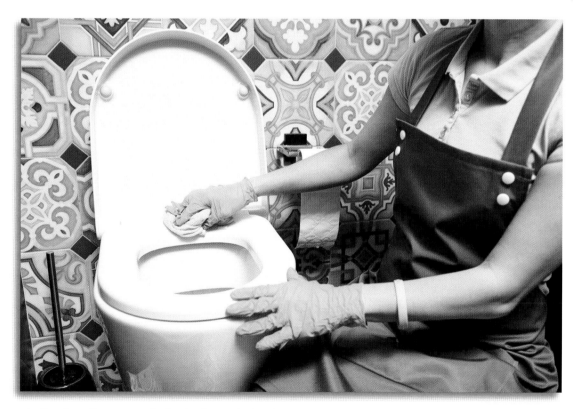

▲ Cleaning toilets may not be fun, but it must be done!

Start Preparing Now

- Practice cleaning your own house: Sweep, mop, make beds, and wash windows. Set times and see if you can get everything done in a few hours.

- Look online and in books to find out proper cleaning techniques, from making a bed to removing stains or cleaning a shower curtain (visit http://www.marthastewart.com for some expert tips).

- Begin collecting cleaning supplies and learn about the effectiveness of various ones.

- Get a part-time job—any job—so you can show prospective employers that you're already a reliable employee.

- Take shop classes so you'll know some basic repair techniques.

- Study basic math—cleaners sometimes need to work with numbers to measure cleaning supplies or run machines.

A housekeeper talks about her job.

Training and How to Get It

Most janitors, maids, and housekeepers don't have any formal training. You won't even need to finish high school, though it will improve your chances of advancement. If you've learned how to clean a house, make beds, wash windows, do dishes, and fold laundry at home then you already have many of the skills you'll need to clean houses.

If you go to work for a cleaning service or janitorial company, you'll learn most of your skills on the job. You'll work with an experienced janitor or housekeeper at first and he or she will teach you the essentials of the job. You'll start with the easiest jobs and gradually move up to more complicated tasks. Many housekeeping companies have training programs to teach you the specific skills you'll need. You'll learn how to sweep and mop, run a vacuum cleaner; and wax, buff, and polish floors. You'll learn about different kinds of cleaners and how to use them safely. You'll learn where to keep your cleaning equipment and supplies and how to stock your rolling cart. Your supervisor will teach you how to collect and dispose of garbage. Some of your training will involve safety and health regulations. A lot of the work that cleaners do could be dangerous if done incorrectly. You'll learn what to do if an accident occurs on the job.

If you work at a hotel, your colleagues or supervisors will teach you how to strip sheets off beds and replace them with new ones, how to hang up towels, and how to clean rooms and bathrooms. You'll have to learn how to tell when you can enter a room and how to speak to guests if you encounter them. After you've worked for a while as a janitor or cleaner, you may learn some basic repair skills. Lots of janitors get training in electricity and plumbing so that they can make simple repairs. If you become a supervisor, you'll attend occasional classes on new cleaning techniques and employee management.

Learn the Lingo

Here are some terms you may hear in the cleaning services field:

- **Grout** The solid gray or white substance between tiles on a floor or wall.

- **Linoleum** A type of flooring made of solid linseed oil and canvas or burlap backing; today vinyl flooring is often incorrectly referred to as linoleum.

- **Laminate flooring** A flooring material made of synthetic materials that looks like natural flooring materials, such as wood or marble; Pergo is a leading brand.

- **Mildew** A fungus that grows on warm, damp surfaces, such as shower curtains.

Finding a Job

Businesses are always looking for cleaners. You can find a job easily by reading your local newspaper's classified section or doing an Internet search for "maid" or "janitor" plus your hometown. You can also go in person to a business where you'd like to work and offer your services. Try maid services, large office buildings, schools, hospitals, or hotels. Another way to find jobs is to contact labor unions or state and local employment service offices.

If you want to clean houses on your own, you can place an online ad in a local town or city message board or in the newspaper classified section, or post fliers at churches or schools, advertising your services as a maid. Word of mouth is a great way to find jobs. If you do a good job ask him or her to spread the word. You can print business cards and give them out as well.

When you speak to a **prospective** employer, be polite, dress neatly, and arrive on time. If you've had other jobs, bring a list of them and include telephone numbers of past employers or clients so that your new boss can call them and ask about you.

Tips for Success

- Attention to detail and directions is key. You may have to remember a long list of cleaning duties. If you do all your tasks well (it's easy to tell if something really is clean or not), you can hope for more and better work.

- Learn to estimate the time it takes to do specific tasks. Once you know this, you can plan with clients and work partners, and you will be able to work with a little less stress because you will know you are running on time.

Reality Check

Cleaning can be dangerous. Back pain and injuries from slipping and falling are common. To avoid injuries, lift heavy objects with your legs, not your back. Use extra care when walking on wet floors, and be aware of power cords and other objects on the floor so you don't trip over them.

LEARN MORE ONLINE

INTERNATIONAL EXECUTIVE HOUSEKEEPERS ASSOCIATION

This association provides benefits such as educational opportunities, conferences, resource materials, and certifications such as "registered executive housekeeper." http://www.ieha.org

MERRY MAIDS

This is one of the biggest maid service companies in the United States. Though the site is primarily directed at potential customers, it includes cleaning tips that could come in handy. http://www.merrymaids.com

Related Jobs to Consider

Food preparation and service worker. As a restaurant worker, you'll perform lots of the same jobs that housekeepers and janitors do, cleaning and organizing your workplace. You'll also cook food and prepare it to be served.

Grounds maintenance worker. You'll work outdoors, mowing lawns, tending gardens, and maintaining outdoor landscape features.

Pest control worker. You'll study the habits of various pests, including roaches, ants, fleas, termites, bees, rats, and mice, and learn how to eradicate them with traps and poisons.

Crime scene (forensics) cleaner. If you have a strong stomach, can follow directions well, and can learn to preserve evidence, you can earn high pay as a forensics cleaner.

How to Move Up

- Become a supervisor or manager of a cleaning team. This will be easiest if you work for a company that has lots of cleaners. You'll definitely need to finish high school or get your general educational development credential (GED) if you want to become a supervisor. A second language, such as Spanish, is particularly useful for managers.

- Become an owner of a cleaning service. You'll hire housekeepers and janitors and send them out to clients. You'll need a good head for business and good people skills.

- Become an executive housekeeper. This position, an actual certification provided to qualifying cleaning supervisors and managers by the International Executive Housekeepers Association, will allow you to manage teams of cleaners at large businesses, such as hospitals or hotels. To become a certified executive housekeeper, you'll have to get an associate's degree in house-keeping from a college, take a 330-hour certification course, or complete a self-study program. Visit http://www.ieha.org for more information.

TEXT-DEPENDENT QUESTIONS

1. *What is the average pay of janitors? Housekeepers?*

2. *How do you find a job in this field?*

3. *What is Pergo?*

4. *What are some related jobs to consider?*

RESEARCH PROJECTS

1. *Find out about green cleaning. What practices does it involve? What kinds of products are available? Why is there increasing interest in green cleaning? You might begin your search at the American Cleaning Institute (http://www.cleaninginstitute.org/), which collects information about a wide variety of safer cleaning products.*

2. *Get experience by cleaning your own home regularly. Better yet, volunteer to help out a neighbor who may be elderly or otherwise have trouble cleaning his or her own house. This way you can start building up referrals.*

Funeral Attendant

*Be part of a funeral team. Prepare the dead
for burial. Comfort the bereaved.*

7

WORDS TO UNDERSTAND

cremate: to burn a dead body.

decomposition: decay.

embalming: a process that preserves a dead body.

People die every day. It's not a pleasant thought, but it's true, and it's also true that every person who dies must be cared for in some way. That's where funeral attendants come in. Funeral attendants work for mortuaries or funeral homes doing essential jobs, some of which involve dead bodies and some of which include more ordinary tasks, such as cleaning, arranging flowers, or setting up chairs. Employees who work in this field find it deeply satisfying. They know they're doing a necessary job and helping the bereaved handle some of the most difficult moments of their lives.

◀ A funeral attendant wears many hats. If a casket needs to be transported, an attendant will drive it in a hearse to the cemetery for burial.

Is This Job Right for You?

To find out if being a funeral attendant is right for you, read the following questions, and answer "Yes" or "No."

Yes	No	**1.**	*Could you be comfortable working around dead bodies?*
Yes	No	**2.**	*Are you comfortable being around people who are crying?*
Yes	No	**3.**	*Are you polite and dignified, and do you dress neatly?*
Yes	No	**4.**	*Are you strong enough to move furniture around?*
Yes	No	**5.**	*Do you enjoy displaying flowers and candles?*
Yes	No	**6.**	*Are you neat and organized?*
Yes	No	**7.**	*Can you follow directions well?*
Yes	No	**8.**	*Do you have an interest in human biology and anatomy?*
Yes	No	**9.**	*Are you sensitive to the needs of other people?*
Yes	No	**10.**	*Are you willing to work weekends and evenings?*

If you answered "Yes" to most of these questions, you have what it takes to make a good funeral attendant. Read on to learn more about this job.

What's the Work Like?

As a funeral attendant, you'll help a funeral director manage funerals, cremation services, and general business. Your duties will include basic housekeeping duties: washing limousines and hearses, cleaning rooms, and setting up and putting away tables, chairs, urns, vases, candles, and other items used during visitations and services. You will have to keep the visitation rooms and possibly a chapel looking nice, decorating them with flowers and polishing the furniture. You may assist the funeral director with paperwork, preparing obituary notices or applying for death certificates. Much of this work is now done online.

Funeral attendants spend lots of time around the dead. You may pick up bodies at the hospital morgue

TALKING MONEY

Funeral attendants averaged $27,110 a year in 2016, according to the U.S. Bureau of Labor Statistics. The highest-paid funeral attendants earned over $39,000 a year. The hourly wage for this job ranged from $8.70 to $19.09.

▲ After a person passes away, the body is often taken to the morgue. If that is the case, it is a funeral attendant's responsibility to retrieve the body and prepare it for viewing or cremation.

or from nursing homes. You'll have to help lift bodies to move them around—from a hospital bed to a stretcher, for instance, or from an **embalming** table into a coffin or casket. If a body must wait more than 24 hours between death and burial, it must be embalmed or refrigerated; you'll wheel bodies in and out of a giant refrigerator on their way to the embalming room or cremation chamber. You may handle the bodies yourself, cleaning them with warm water and soap, and helping the embalmer prepare them properly. You may dress bodies and put them into their coffins. You may

TALKING TRENDS

In 2016, there were more than 35,000 funeral attendants working in the United States. The field isn't growing rapidly—the Bureau of Labor Statistics projects that the funeral industry will grow at about an average rate in the next 10 years.

▲ Wakes and funerals can be a very emotional time for the friends and family of the deceased. The funeral attendant needs to be there for them in their grief and assist them with anything they may need.

be in charge of funeral equipment, such as stretchers and lowering straps (used to lower coffins into graves).

Today about half of the deceased are **cremated**. You may likely help cremate bodies, placing them in a casket or container that is then put in a cremation chamber, an oven that reaches temperatures of 1,400°F to 1,800°F. After the ashes cool, you'll carefully remove them and place them in a container for the family; some families save the ashes in an urn, while others scatter them in some symbolic location.

As a funeral attendant, you'll see lots of grieving people. You'll speak to them kindly and make their difficult time a little bit easier. You may help them choose caskets or urns and plan funeral services for their loved ones. You'll help older people in and out of limousines and walk them to chairs in the visitation room. You may find family members crying on your shoulder.

Who's Hiring?

- A smaller family-owned funeral home

- A larger "regional partner" funeral home

Where Are the Jobs?

You'll do most of your work in the funeral home. Some of your day will be spent in visitation rooms and chapels; you'll have to dress somewhat formally and speak in a quiet, polite voice when mourners are present. You may spend time in the embalming room. That's where the embalmer prepares the body for view and burial or cremation, for instance, by replacing bodily fluids with embalming fluid to prevent rapid **decomposition** . You'll wear protective clothing and gloves to keep fluids from touching your body when you touch the dead person. The smells can sometimes be strong—you'd better have an iron stomach. You may also enter the funeral home's giant refrigerator where it stores unembalmed bodies or the room that houses its cremation chamber.

Your work may take you beyond the confines of the funeral home. You may drive a hearse to pick up bodies from the hospital morgue or to deliver bodies to the cemetery. Sometimes families want to hold funerals at synagogues, other houses of worship, or personally meaningful sites. You'll spend some of your time at cemeteries, helping to carry coffins as a pallbearer or standing quietly to show your respect during funerals and memorial services.

▲ A funeral attendant meets with a family as they make decisions for a funeral.

A Typical Day

Here are the highlights of a typical day for a funeral attendant.

Hold a morning conference. You greet a pair of customers: a woman whose elderly husband has died and their daughter. You first show them into the casket display room so they can see the available caskets. You then escort them into the funeral director's office and sit down as they convey their requests to the funeral director. The deceased was a Korean War veteran who liked 1950s rock and roll music; the director asks you to assemble a playlist of his favorite songs to play during the service.

Prepare the deceased. After the customers leave, you and the funeral director begin a cremation, placing a body in the cremation chamber. Later that morning, you help the embalmer prepare a body, cleaning it, helping embalm it, dressing the person, and laying him in the casket. The cremation is now finished; you remove the remains from the cremation chamber and place them in an urn.

Watch a tour of a funeral home.

Set up for viewing. You sweep and vacuum the viewing room and set up chairs for a visitation. You wheel in the casket and open the lid to reveal the deceased. You arrange flowers and personal items from the deceased on and around the casket and turn on music. When guests start arriving, you greet them at the door and show them in.

Start Preparing Now

- Take classes in biology and chemistry.

- Take a psychology class to understand how people sort through their emotions.

- Practice being a good listener.

- Practice good manners and courteous public speaking.

- Find a summer job or internship in a funeral home.

- Volunteer at a nursing home—you'll be around lots of elderly people and will see how family members react when someone dies.

Training and How to Get It

Before you become a full-time funeral attendant, you'll probably want to graduate from high school (a high school diploma isn't necessary, but is recommended) and to have a driver's license. Depending on your state, you may need to be trained in how to handle blood and avoid catching diseases from dead bodies. Your prospective employer will probably run a criminal background check on you. Some states require funeral directors to pay a fee to register each funeral attendant working for them as licensed funeral attendants. However, in most cases a license is not necessary, and as a funeral attendant you will not be required to register yourself. The registration requirements are meant to ensure that all funeral attendants are properly supervised. Check out the National Funeral Directors Association Web site for information on licensing requirements for funeral workers in each state.

Much of the work you'll do as a funeral attendant is a matter of common sense, and you can gain the specific training you need on the job. At work, you'll also study the various types and costs of coffins and urns and learn how to help mourners choose them. You may learn

▲ Funeral attendants help loved ones decide which coffin to choose, guiding them to what is affordable and reasonable.

how to drive a hearse or van. You'll learn how to move a dead body from place to place, how to open and close coffins at appropriate points in a service, and how to get coffins into graves or crypts by using lifts or straps. You may learn how to cremate bodies and handle the ashes. You'll learn how to prepare a grave and graveside for a funeral. Your employer may teach you how to speak to mourners and how to help them in and out of limousines. He or she will also teach you how to prepare viewing rooms and chapels, setting up chairs and placing candles and flowers. You need to know how to sweep, vacuum, and mop, and how to dust and polish furniture. You may learn the basics of arranging flowers for funeral services.

Finding a Job

Look for advertisements in the local newspaper or on the Internet. You can find local opportunities by doing an Internet search for "funeral attendant" or "mortuary assistant" plus your hometown. You can also look on job search Web sites such as Monster.com. One of the best ways to find a job as a funeral attendant is to go to a funeral home and offer your services. Often jobs are not advertised, but a funeral director may be happy to hire a good worker. Bring your high school transcript and a résumé that includes information about any jobs you've had. Dress conservatively and be on your best behavior. Remember the funeral director will want to know how you'll act around mourners. If the funeral director schedules an interview with you, show up on time. Impress the director with your enthusiasm, responsibility, and dignity.

Often attendants start working for funeral homes part time in high school. If you're still in high school, this might be a good way to find out if a career in funeral services would suit you.

Learn the Lingo

Here are some terms you hear working as a funeral attendant:

- **Hearse** A large car that carries coffins to and from funerals.
- **Mortuary science** The study of funerals, including embalming techniques, human physiology, cremation, state laws, and grief counseling. You can study for such a program at college or at a private mortuary school.

Tips for Success

- According to the National Funeral Directors Association (NFDA), families want personalized funerals that celebrate the individuality of the deceased. You'll be a valuable asset if you can

NOTES FROM THE FIELD

Certified funeral attendant, *Baileyville, Maine*

Q: *How did you get your job?*

A: After I delivered eulogies and served as a pallbearer at some friends' funerals, a local funeral director mentioned the fact that I seemed relatively comfortable working with the deceased's family members as well as the deceased. He asked me if I'd ever considered becoming a licensed funeral attendant and working part time for him. So, that's exactly what I did and have really enjoyed it.

Q: *What do you like best about your job?*

A: Lots! There are so many myths out there about working with the dead and all sorts of horrible and terrible things going on during the preparation process. I enjoy clarifying those rumors. I like to explain that deceased folks are treated with respect and love while being prepared for viewing, cremation, or whatever the circumstance might be. For example, I massage the head and hands of the person being embalmed to recirculate and stimulate color and bring back appearance as best as can be expected. I always think of the person being someone I love and care about.

Q: *What's the most challenging part of your job?*

A: It's so tough to see people in [emotional] pain. It's hard not show your own feelings when a parent has lost a child, or anyone for that matter. There never is a right or correct thing to say to make someone feel better. Sometimes just to be there with a great set of ears and an ever-ready hug is a part of what folks need.

Q: *What are the keys to success to being a funeral attendant?*

A: Flexibility. It's tough to be ready at a minute's notice. The director might call me at two in the morning. Within a minute's notice I must be dressed in my suit, presentable, and ready to claim a body at a hospital, enter the scene of a suicide, or retrieve the remains of a car accident victim. Composure is a must.

help customize a service, such as by preparing Webcasts of services, or putting together a slide show of the key moments in the person's life to be shown during the funeral.

- Funerals are time-sensitive, and you need to be very well informed about your own use of time. Did you place a timely call for flowers or any catering needs? If you tell someone you can perform a certain task with the body of the deceased in a certain amount of time, you need to be able to do it—or keep your supervisor posted as to any complications.

LEARN MORE ONLINE

AMERICAN SOCIETY OF EMBALMERS
This site has lots of information about working in the funeral industry, and of course, about embalming. http://amsocembalmers.org/

NATIONAL FUNERAL DIRECTORS ASSOCIATION
This is the largest association of funeral directors in the country. http://www.nfda.org

Reality Check

It's hard to be around death every day. As a funeral attendant, you'll see the bodies of people who have died in gruesome ways, and you'll hear the stories of people who have died tragically. You'll have to learn how to handle the emotions that will arise from your work. Funeral workers do sometimes break down and cry, but the best ones manage to keep the tears back until the mourners have left.

Related Jobs to Consider

Cosmetologist. Though most cosmetologists work on living people, a few work for funeral homes helping to prepare the dead for viewing during a funeral. In addition to applying makeup, you might also fix the hair of the dead.

Floral designer. If you like flowers but don't like funerals, become a floral designer. You'll spend your days arranging flowers—sometimes for funerals, but also for happy occasions like weddings and proms.

EMT or paramedic. If you have a strong stomach and want to help people, but yearn for more action than you may see as a funeral home attendant, consider a career as an emergency medical technician or paramedic.

How to Move Up

• Become an embalmer. You'll prepare bodies for burial by replacing their body fluids with embalming fluid. You'll need to study embalming at mortuary school or college and pass an exam to get certified.

• Become a funeral director. If you earn a college degree (bachelor's or associate's) in mortuary science, serve a one-year apprenticeship, and pass a state licensing exam (these requirements vary somewhat by state), you can manage a funeral home.

• Become a social worker. This isn't directly related to funeral work, but social workers handle many of the same emotional situations that funeral attendants encounter—death, dying, and grieving survivors.

TEXT-DEPENDENT QUESTIONS

1. *What duties does a funeral attendant do?*

2. *What training does the job require?*

3. *What is mortuary science?*

4. *How do you move up in this field?*

RESEARCH PROJECTS

1. *Choose a culture that's different from your own and research their customs surrounding death. It could be an ancient culture, such as the Greeks or Egyptians, or a contemporary one. How did (or does) the culture respond to death? What customs does the culture observe, and why did those customs evolve the way they did?*

2. *Explore the Web site of the Order of the Good Death, a group of funeral directors and workers who support a more "open, honest engagement with death" (http://www.orderofthegooddeath.com/).*

Seamstress/Tailor/ Upholsterer

8

Alter clothes to fit perfectly. Make custom clothing. Make old fabric-covered furniture look like new

WORDS TO UNDERSTAND

alterations: here, adjustments made to clothes to make them fit better.

apprentice: a trainee.

textile: a fabric.

Do you love the look and feel of fabric? Does the construction of clothing or fabric-covered furniture interest you? Do you like the smell of new car seats? And are you good with your hands? If so, you should consider a career in one of the sewing professions. Seamstresses and tailors make custom clothing and perform **alterations** to make off-the-rack clothes fit perfectly. Upholsterers sew cloth and leather covers for furniture and car seats and install them on top of springs and cushioning. Though in general the sewing professions are in something of a decline, shows like *Project Runway* are capturing a huge audience, and with new custom-pattern software making custom clothing more available to ordinary people, interest in jobs related to clothing design appear to be on

◀ Designing custom clothes and furniture is an art in itself. Seamstresses, tailors, and upholsterers create and alter clothing and furniture, bringing their designs to life with different fabrics.

the upswing. There's definitely a demand for people with the skill to make custom clothing and furniture.

Is This Job Right for You?

To find out if being a tailor, seamstress, or upholsterer is right for you, read each of the following questions and answer "Yes" or "No."

Yes	No	**1.**	*Do you like working with your hands?*
Yes	No	**2.**	*Do you have good manual dexterity?*
Yes	No	**3.**	*Are you strong (for upholsterers)?*
Yes	No	**4.**	*Can you sit still for hours?*
Yes	No	**5.**	*Do you have good eyesight?*
Yes	No	**6.**	*Do you like to look at and handle cloth?*
Yes	No	**7.**	*Do you like to look at clothing or furniture?*
Yes	No	**8.**	*Can you work independently?*
Yes	No	**9.**	*Can you measure things precisely?*
Yes	No	**10.**	*Are you a perfectionist?*

If you answered "Yes" to most of these questions, you may have the talent to pursue a career as a seamstress, tailor, or upholsterer. To find out more about these jobs, read on.

What's the Work Like?

If you become a seamstress or tailor, you'll make and repair clothing for customers. Tailors are generally thought of as being male and making clothing for men, and seamstresses or dressmakers are typically female and mostly create clothing for women. However, the difference today is becoming irrelevant. As a tailor or seamstress, much of your work will be alterations of off-the-rack garments. You'll do some of the alterations by hand and some with a sewing machine. Some customers will want you to sew new

TALKING MONEY

The average income for tailors, dressmakers, and custom sewers is about $28,000 per year, according to the U.S. Bureau of Labor Statistics. But the highest earners made over $46,000 a year. Upholsterers earned an average income of about $33,000, though the highest-paid earned over $52,000.

▲ A tailor creates a pattern based on a customer's measurements to make a custom shirt.

garments for them using lengths of fabric and patterns. You may even create your own patterns and garment designs, either by hand or by using new computer programs that generate patterns based on your clients' measurements. Some seamstresses and tailors specialize in costumes for theaters and film studios. Others make items such as custom curtains.

Seamstresses and tailors are considered custom sewers. Another type of sewing worker works in a factory; in larger factories they may work as sewing machine operators, **textile** cutting machine setters, or pattern makers. The pay can be about the same, but if you work in a factory, you'll be making large numbers of the same mass-produced garments instead of custom garments.

▲ Factories around the world mass produce clothing. Here, a man working in a clothing factory operates a laser machine to cut and engrave materials.

As an upholsterer, you'll make and repair furniture that is covered with fabric and padding. You may also upholster car seats in leather or cloth. To make a new piece of furniture, you'll start with a wooden frame (probably made by someone else). You'll stretch webbing over it, tack it down tight, and attach springs. You'll cover the springs with padding or stuffing to make a soft surface. You'll then cut out pieces of fabric, sew them together, and glue or tack them over the padding. You may add decorations such as ribbon or buttons. To fix furniture, you'll rip out old fabric and stuffing, reglue the frame where it has come loose, and replace any portions of the webbing and springs that have worn out. Then you'll cover the springs with padding and the cloth covers you have cut and sewn together. You may help customers choose fabric based on pattern, texture, and price. You may deliver finished pieces to your customers. You may upholster car interiors, in addition to furniture.

Who's Hiring?

- A clothing store

- An alterations shop

- A costume shop

- A theater

- A fashion or apparel designer

- A dry cleaner

- A furniture store

- A furniture repair shop

- An automobile upholstery shop

- Yourself

Where Are the Jobs?

As a tailor or seamstress, you may work in an alterations shop or in the alterations department of a clothing store. You'll do your work sitting at a table that contains your sewing machine, needles and thread, pins, scissors, measuring tape, and other pieces of equipment. When you fit clothes on customers, you'll have them stand on a raised box in front of a mirror. This gives you access to their feet and allows them to see how the garments look on them.

As an upholsterer, you may work in a furniture factory or a furniture repair shop. You'll work in a room that has enough space to store and manipulate big pieces of furniture, such as couches, and possibly bolts of fabric. You may do some work in a garage that can hold vehicles. You'll probably do some of your work sitting or squatting on the floor, and sometimes you'll have to stand up for long periods of time. You may spend some of your time in a delivery van, picking up and dropping off pieces of furniture. Many upholsterers, tailors, and seamstresses work at home. Of course, you'll need a room big enough to hold your sewing or upholstering equipment.

TALKING TRENDS

In 2016 in the United States, about 21,000 people worked as tailors or dressmakers and about 32,000 worked as upholsterers. The number of positions in both fields has been declining, but some experts predict that given the do-it-yourself craze, the increased popularity of fashion design may create a resurgence in the field.

A Typical Day

Here are highlights of a typical day for a seamstress.

Mark for alterations. A high school student comes in with several cheerleading uniforms that she inherited from a classmate who has graduated. The uniforms are much too big for their current owner. You fold and pin them so that they'll fit properly and tell her to pick them up in a week.

Bead a wedding dress. A client wants the hem of her wedding dress decorated with rhinestones and pearls. You spend two hours working on this but don't finish. This job will take several days to complete.

Make a cape. Another client has brought you a pattern and fabric to make a cape for her son's Halloween costume. You lay the cloth out on the pattern, cut out the pieces, and quickly run them together on your sewing machine.

▲ In order to alter clothing or create a new garment, a tailor or seamstress must take precise measurements to make sure it will fit properly.

Start Preparing Now

- Take art classes. Learn about line and color. Practice drawing.

- Take classes in sewing or upholstery.

- Practice sewing. Hem or alter your clothes, or sew your own clothes from patterns. Try to stitch both by hand and on your machine.

- Examine the construction of your own clothes and of clothes in stores to learn about quality.

- Visit fabric stores to examine fabrics.

- Do the laundry and see what it does to clothes.

Training and How to Get It

Custom sewing and upholstery are both skilled trades that require a great deal of training to master. You'll have to learn how to take measurements, cut cloth to a pattern, and sew, both by hand and by machine. You'll also need to understand the properties of various kinds of cloth. You don't need any particular certification or license to enter a sewing field, but you will have to spend a lot of time learning your trade.

If you want to become an upholsterer, you can expect to spend several years learning your skills. Most upholsterers learn the trade on the job, working as assistants in upholstery shops. You might be able to find an upholsterer to take you on as an apprentice; if you do this, be sure to work out the details of the apprenticeship before you sign a contract. The same applies to dressmaking and tailoring. Most people learn their skills on the job. Many sewing professionals first learned to sew at home with family members. Others train as apprentices or assistants in shops.

If you want to advance, it's a good idea to have some formal training. Your high school may offer classes in sewing or upholstery. Some community and technical colleges offer certification programs in dressmaking, tailoring, and furniture or automotive upholstery; some automotive upholstery programs include training in glass repair as well. An Internet search for your hometown plus "upholstery program" or "upholstery certification" can locate upholstery programs. For custom sewing, search for "dressmaking training" or "tailoring." You can also call technical colleges in your area to ask about programs.

NOTES FROM THE FIELD

Upholsterer, *Vadnais Heights, Minnesota*

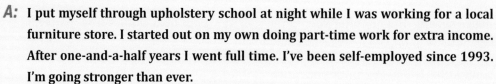

Q: *How did you get your job?*

A: I put myself through upholstery school at night while I was working for a local furniture store. I started out on my own doing part-time work for extra income. After one-and-a-half years I went full time. I've been self-employed since 1993. I'm going stronger than ever.

Q: *What do you like best about your job?*

A: I like making people's dreams come true and seeing their ideas brought to life by doing things like upholstering family heirlooms or building a custom street rod interior from scratch. It is rewarding to be able to do this work for a living.

Q: *What's the most challenging part of your job?*

A: Working with the various personalities of customers can be very challenging. Getting the work done on time is also hard, as you never know exactly how long something will take until you are halfway through it.

Q: *What are the keys to success to being an upholsterer?*

A: Quality is of the utmost to being successful in this field—not just meeting the customer's expectations but exceeding them. You have to be able to estimate jobs accurately and be well organized.

Training programs cover fibers, fabrics, cutting cloth, altering patterns, and finishing work. A certification or associate's degree in the field will make you more marketable because employers will see that you already know basic skills. However you start, you should expect to spend years mastering your craft. You can learn enough to do basic upholstery and simple custom sewing in a few weeks, but it can take 8 to 10 years to learn how to do the finest custom work.

Learn the Lingo

Here are a few words you'll hear as a seamstress, tailor, or upholsterer:

- **Garment** An item of clothing. The field of clothing manufacture is also called the "garment industry."

See what a high-end tailor's job is like.

- **Interfacing** A layer of cloth sewn inside the main fabric of a garment to help support the garment in a high-stress area, such as a collar or waistband.

- **Seam** A line of stitches that joins two pieces of fabric together.

- **Welt pocket** A pocket with one or two "lips."

Finding a Job

Most businesses that hire seamstresses, tailors, or upholsterers want experienced workers who know at least the basics of the trade. You'll have a much easier time finding work if you already know how to sew or have begun to study upholstery. If you don't have any experience, however, don't let that stop you from looking for work because most workers in the sewing trades learn most of their craft on the job. It just may be harder for you to find a job, and your starting pay will probably be lower.

To find job opportunities, read the newspaper classified ads or conduct an Internet search for the name of your hometown plus "seamstress" or "upholsterer." You can also go directly to alteration shops, dry cleaners, furniture repair shops, or other places that hire seamstresses or upholsterers and offer your services. If you get an interview, be sure to show up on time! Be polite and enthusiastic, and dress neatly. Bring along a copy of your résumé. If you've already sewn some garments, bring them along to show your prospective employer.

Tips for Success

- Attention to detail is key. People arc very picky about how their clothes look and fit or about the smoothness of their furniture or car seats. Take your time to do the job right.

- Learn how long it takes you to do specific tasks—putting the buttons on a shirt, hemming a dress, or taking in a jacket. You will learn what you need to do faster so that it pays to do the work, and you will also start being able to plan your work schedule.

▲ Whether working with fabric or leather, an upholsterer must ensure that the material is taut and free of wrinkles.

Reality Check

Work carefully to avoid injuries! Seamstresses and upholsterers get lots of aches and pains from bending over their work. Repetitive stress injuries, such as carpal tunnel syndrome, are common. And watch out for those sharp needles and scissors!

Related Jobs to Consider

Textile machine operator or tender. You'll work in a textile factory making fibers such as cotton, rayon, or fiberglass, and then transforming them into cloth on knitting or weaving machines.

Sewing machine operator. You'll sew together the pieces of garments for a mass clothing manufacturer.

Pattern maker. You'll work with a clothing designer to convert his or her designs into patterns of various sizes so that a factory can produce a large number of the same garment.

Shoe or leather worker. You'll work in a factory or shoe repair shop assembling shoes and bags made of leather, canvas, or plastic.

Clothing salesperson. You'll help customers choose clothing that fits well, and possibly mark new clothes for alteration.

Drapery maker. You'll specialize in sewing drapes and creating window treatments for your clients.

How to Move Up

- Become a shop supervisor. As a manager, you'll command a higher salary than a seamstress or upholsterer.

- Open your own shop. As a tailor, dressmaker, or custom upholsterer, running your own business will allow you to choose your jobs and earn more money. You should learn the basics of running a business before you try this.

- Become a fashion designer. You'll need to go to college to study fashion design, but a background in sewing is essential.

LEARN MORE ONLINE

LIVINGSOFT NORTHWEST

A site that sells custom patterns made to individual measurements. http://www.livingsoftnw.com

PROFESSIONAL ASSOCIATION OF CUSTOM CLOTHIERS

This is an association of tailors, dressmakers, pattern makers, and various other sewing professionals. It has a list of schools that teach sewing and design skills. http://www.paccprofessionals.org

UPHOLSTER MAGAZINE ONLINE

This magazine publishes articles on upholstery, detailed instructions on upholstery techniques, and a discussion board on upholstery topics. http://www.upholster.com

TEXT-DEPENDENT QUESTIONS

1. *What types of tasks does a tailor do?*

2. *What types of tasks does an upholsterer do?*

3. *Who hires people in these jobs?*

4. *What are some related jobs you could consider?*

1. *Find a sewing class near you by searching online for "sewing class" and your location. Craft stores like JoAnn's often offer classes for little or no money.*

2. *Practice your sewing skills with a sewing machine or, if you don't have access to one, by hand-stitching. You can find sewing projects on craft-related sites like Pinterest. The Hobby Lobby site also features instructions and videos for do-it-yourself projects (https://www.hobbylobby.com/DIY-Projects-Videos/c/13).*

▲ As an upholsterer, you'll make and repair furniture that is covered with fabric and padding. You may also upholster car seats in leather or cloth.

INDEX

PHOTO CREDITS